POLITICAL REFORM LEADERS IN EASTERN EUROPE AND THE FORMER SOVIET UNION

GLOBAL PROFILES

POLITICAL REFORM LEADERS IN EASTERN EUROPE AND THE FORMER SOVIET UNION

Patrick Austin Tracey

Facts On File, Inc.

Political Reform Leaders in Eastern Europe and the Former Soviet Union

Copyright © 1997 by Patrick Austin Tracey

All rights reserved. No part of this book may be reproduced or utilized in any form or by any means, electronic or mechanical, including photocopying, recording, or by any information storage or retrieval systems, without permission in writing from the publisher. For information contact:

Facts On File, Inc.
11 Penn Plaza
New York NY 10001

Library of Congress Cataloging-in-Publication Data

Tracey, Patrick Austin.
   Political reform leaders in Eastern Europe and the former Soviet Union / by Patrick Austin Tracey.
     p. cm. — (Global profiles)
   Includes bibliographical references and index.
   Summary: Profiles eight leaders for their attempts to introduce functional democracy in their respective countries: Andrei Sakharov, Alexander Dubcek, Boris Yeltsin, Mikhail Gorbachev, Vaclav Havel, Lech Walesa, Father Jerzy Popieluszko, and Pastor Laszlo Tokes.
   ISBN 0-8160-3129-0 (alk. paper)
   1. Europe, Eastern—Politics and government—1989—Juvenile literature. 2. Russia (Federation)—Politics and government—Juvenile literature. 3. Politicians—Europe, Eastern—Biography—Juvenile literature. 4. Reformers—Europe, Eastern—Biography—Juvenile literature. 5. Politicians—Russia (Federation)—Biography—Juvenile literature. 6. Reformers—Russia (Federation)—Biography—Juvenile literature. [1. Europe, Eastern—Politics and government. 2. Russia (Federation)—Politics and government. 3. Reformers. 4. Politicians.] I. Title. II. Series.
DJK51.T7 1996
947'.00099—dc20   95-25502

Facts On File books are available at special discounts when purchased in bulk quantities for businesses, associations, institutions or sales promotions. Please call our Special Sales Department in New York at 212/967-8800 or 800/322-8755.

Text design by Catherine Rincon Hyman
Cover design by Nora Wertz
Front cover photographs: AP/Wide World Photos

This book is printed on acid-free paper.

Printed in the United States of America

MP FOF 10 9 8 7 6 5 4 3 2 1

To Barbara,

for teaching me that

love is patience.

Contents

Introduction	ix
Andrei Sakharov	1
Alexander Dubcek	21
Boris Yeltsin	41
Mikhail Gorbachev	63
Vaclav Havel	83
Lech Walesa	107
Father Jerzy Popieluszko	129
Pastor Laszlo Tokes	151
Index	173

Introduction

DEMOCRATIC REFORMERS IN EASTERN EUROPE AND THE FORMER SOVIET UNION

Certain years go down in history as landmarks. Such a year was 1989, a year that will always be remembered for the ending of orthodox communism. As the 1980s drew to a close, a mood of democratic reform that had already swept the Soviet Union triggered a chain reaction of political upheavals elsewhere in Eastern Europe—and culminated in real freedom for one sixth of the world's population. Caught up in the tumult were thousands of individuals who made great sacrifices—but those featured in this book played the most pivotal roles in toppling nearly a century of Communist rule.

What follows is the story of these leaders. All eight were truly remarkable men. To them, freedom was a necessity of life, synonymous with existence itself, and they would dedicate their lives to gaining freedom for their countrymen.

It is certain that none of the democratic revolutions in Eastern Europe would have occurred as soon as they did if these eight men had not led the way. Without their determination, there is little doubt indeed that the iron fist of

Stalinism-Leninism would still be gripping the Soviet Union and the satellite states in Eastern Europe today.

They were all, in a sense, infants in the struggle for democracy. And like infants, they seemed oblivious to danger to themselves. They were willing to risk death, imprisonment, or loss of office. They had a natural trust and a touching faith in the unseen forces of goodness that would miraculously prevail. To them, democracy was a consuming flame, worth any sacrifice—and they were equal to the challenge.

Some were insiders—Communist Party officials themselves who, quite paradoxically, launched their careers with strong faith in the promise of the Communist ideology and then worked for change from within the established channels of government. Three men in particular—Alexander Dubcek in Czechoslovakia and later Mikhail Gorbachev and Boris Yeltsin in the Soviet Union—were career politicians who enjoyed all the perks and privileges that top Communist Party stature confers. Somehow they were picked by their peers to preside over the conservative, self-protective power structures and went on to affect change from within. It was remarkable that they were chosen at all by the party functionaries—men who routinely quashed anything that smacked of political deviation.

Others were pure outsiders—dissidents who for decades kicked at the struts of power and were punished severely by imprisonment, internal exile, joblessness, and harassment by government police. Still they stood out from the faceless populace, and stood up to gigantic governments whose leaders had habitually hidden behind intimidation and lies. Their lives plunged periodically from the heights of supreme optimism and blind faith to the depths of sarcastic cynicism. Ultimately, they rose above circumstance to make enormous contributions. Of the five dissidents in this book, two went on to win presidencies.

Some of these heroes are more well known than others. Soviet leader Mikhail Gorbachev, for instance, attained a level of international popularity enjoyed by few people in this century. Like so many others in history who were swallowed by their own revolutions, however, Gorbachev has faded into relative obscurity, a man now widely disliked in his own country despite the great forces of freedom that he, more than anyone, unleashed on the world stage. So, too, was Lech Walesa fated to a dramatic rise and fall. Since his defeat in the last presidential elections in Poland, Walesa has returned to his old job as a shipyard electrician.

Whatever their individual achievements, the greatness of the epic struggles of heroes will always be acknowledged, in their own countries and beyond the seas. What was most remarkable about them all is that none ever resorted to violence. With the exception of Romania, where the Communist regime reacted brutally, the democratic revolutions were bloodless, proving once again what political scientists have long maintained: Real revolutionary movements seldom take power by violence.

Political scientists also define revolutions as those movements that produce far-reaching changes in the way people live. Certainly by that definition the leaders profiled in this book are true revolutionaries, for their labors have given birth to entirely new political institutions, and to a number of basic cultural, social, and economic changes in their countries as well. Whether the fledgling democracies they hatched will survive depends entirely on how they are nourished.

If to sustain a democracy it is necessary to remember where that democracy came from, then it is urgently necessary to ask where our heroes' notions of reform originated. What intellectual and biographical influences shaped their thinking? None of them was perfect; nobody is. Sometimes they frolicked like clumsy clowns, with an irresponsible disregard for the future. Yet in every case, when they strayed off center, they seemed to have an internal compass that pointed them back on track.

And how had such strong iconoclasts risen to prominence in countries that placed a premium on conformity, that had tried above all else to grind down the individuality of their people? There is no doubt that they all had uncanny political instincts. They knew when to pull back—when the chilling grip of Communist authoritarianism grew more insistent. And they knew when to take the offensive. Time and again, they underwent sharp disappointments. Often they had to sit patiently, resigned to the knowledge that sheer idealism is impractical. And so they waited, biding their time with quiet confidence and anticipation.

Certainly each was possessed of strong beliefs—strong enough to enable them to be candid about the failures within communism. They also shared the traits of patience, determination and flexibility. Above all, they were willing to speak the truth, to be unafraid, and to stand up for themselves under any circumstances. It is said that fear weakens a person, and that it is necessary to face fear with bravery, which in the end will conquer fear. The profiles that follow are living monuments to that wisdom—to the heart-tugging innocence and wonder, blind faith, and raw courage of a small group of reform-minded leaders.

Once they emerge as leaders, it is easier to see some of the traits that cast these men in grander molds, that forged different and finer metal than most ordinary citizens are made of. Yet it seems as though most of these men gathered self-survival instincts from the harshness and suspicion of their childhoods. Those terrors were very real to people living behind the Iron Curtain.

The hardships engulfed the early years of their childhood and were far more devastating than the outside world could imagine. The depravations forged not only a resilience and self-assurance in these men, but also an ability to thrive on crisis itself. Survival became a near obsession, a dogged determination to survive.

In many cases it was the idealism of youth that stirred their hearts and set their blood afire against the stifling authority of repressive governments. For when poverty and lack of opportunity impede at every turn, one must be willing to find a way around life's obstacles. When a system of government offers no chance for meaningful change and advancement, those opportunities must be seized.

Obviously, in the selection of subjects, I have tried to choose the most successful figures—those who played major roles in spearheading the political reform movements in each country. Each chapter focuses on a single individual, describing his varying degrees of success or failure. Each profile emphasizes the special qualities of leadership of these figures, the qualities that inspired millions of others to follow in their footsteps.

It is hoped that their biographies will also serve as a primer for the times they've lived in. While their individual experiences with Communist rule were distinct, most were outspoken even before the changes in the Soviet Union produced a climate for truly radical change.

Above all it is hoped that readers will gain a solid understanding of what made these leaders tick—that is, the common experiences they shared, the similar challenges they met, and the way each, in his own inimitable way, chose to meet such hurdles. If the book succeeds, it does so to the extent that readers see something new in each of these biographies, making the collection more than just another rehashing of the changes in Eastern Europe and the former Soviet Union from a strictly political viewpoint.

Andrei Sakharov, the Nobel Prize–winning physicist, poses near his home-in-exile. (AP/Wide World Photos)

Andrei Sakharov

When Andrei Sakharov developed the world's first hydrogen bomb, the Soviet Union trumpeted his accomplishment proudly. He'd given his country its first incontestable edge in the nuclear arms race with the United States—and a public relations coup of the first order. The notoriety weighed heavily on the young scientist. He recognized that the mere existence of nuclear weapons posed a threat of global extinction, and he felt a keen responsibility to speak out against them.

At first the Soviet authorities puzzled over how to respond to these criticisms, especially since they came from the scientist who had been so instrumental in the creation of nuclear weapons. Sakharov had also become one of the Soviet Union's most heralded citizens. The Politburo could hardly expel him, if only because his intimate knowledge of the Soviet weapons programs could jeopardize national security. But in 1980, when the disillusioned "father of the hydrogen bomb" dared to condemn the invasion of Afghanistan as immoral and a product of Soviet expansionism, he was sentenced to internal exile in Gorki, a few hundred miles east of Moscow.

Sakharov and his wife were condemned by the Soviet authorities and vilified by the Soviet press, but still they refused to be silenced. As a result, the man who for 20 years had been the key figure in the Soviet nuclear

> weapons program would become one of the world's most outspoken moral voices against totalitarianism and the threat of nuclear extinction.

Andrei Sakharov was born May 21, 1921, to Dmitri Sakharov—a well-known physics teacher—and Yekaterina Sofiano—a God-fearing woman of Russianized Greek heritage—in a maternity hospital outside of Moscow. For the first year of his life, the family lived in a small basement apartment. Andrei was an easy-going baby, though it had been a difficult birth, and for some unknown reason he could not even raise his head for several months.

When Andrei was still an infant the family moved in with his paternal grandparents in Moscow on Granatny Lane. This home would serve as a refuge to an extended Sakharov family during the bloody civil war that followed the Bolshevik Revolution.

Andrei cherished the time spent with his grandmother. She'd taught herself English, and would often read aloud to him from the family Bible. It was from his grandmother that the young boy would come to gain an appreciation for English literature. Yet it was Andrei's father, a physicist, who had the biggest influence on him. An author of several volumes on physics, the senior Sakharov had written the standard physics text for Russian secondary school students. At the age of six Andrei began a program of private tutoring in all subjects. He spent hours at a time in his father's cramped, book-filled study, watching him work late into the night. By age 12 Andrei was immersing himself in the study of physics. Dmitri Sakharov had recognized his son's genius when he was a very young boy and strongly encouraged Andrei's education.

Andrei recalled this period of early adolescence as a great boon to his intellectual development. He was especially drawn to physics. What fascinated him more than anything else was the possibility of being able to use math and science to reduce the whole natural world to the precise interactions of tiny atoms.

Enrolled in public school at age 13, Andrei was introverted and shy with his classmates, but because he had already mastered most of his high school lessons, he found plenty of time to continue with his experiments at home. Proving his intellectual abilities at an early age, Andrei graduated as one of two honors students in his class, which exempted him from the college entrance examination.

In 1938 he enrolled at Moscow State University. He had little trouble with his assignments, breezing through everything except his courses in Marxism-Leninism. Sakharov did not question the ideologies themselves, which predicted the coming of a new industrial order in which the laboring class would achieve preeminence over the capitalist class. But he did feel that these philosophies tended to overlook advances already made by modern science, such as evolutionary theory. He approached even Karl Marx's classic opus, *Das Kapital*, with the same disdain he would one day express for Soviet bureaucracy. "The very size of the book put me off," he once wrote.

Nevertheless, Sakharov thought Marx's brand of socialism was probably humanity's best chance for alleviating human suffering, in theory if not in practice. And he was dedicated to his country—so much so that Sakharov desperately wanted to fight for its defense during World War II, especially after the Germans invaded in June of 1942. As a promising young scientist, however, he had already been moved away to Ashkabad, near the Iranian border, where the physics department was resettled and he could continue his work in physics. In Ashkabad, Sakharov still had to contend with the crowded living quarters and meager food rations of the wartime economy.

Every day he listened closely to radio reports of the battles with the Germans. One day Sakharov learned that his family's home on Granatny Lane had been destroyed by a shell. Surprisingly, no one was injured.

When he finished his exams in 1942, Sakharov had a chance to play a more direct role in the war. At a munitions factory on the Volga River he was assigned to the chief mechanic's office. There he developed several inventions to improve quality control procedures. He also met and married his first wife, Klava Vikhireva.

A local girl who had been a student in Leningrad, Klava had returned home during the war to work as a lab assistant in the chemical department. During the war years the young newlyweds lived with Klava's parents in a workers' housing settlement near the Volga. Sakharov helped farm on the family's plot of land, which they used to earn some extra income by selling any surplus food they could spare.

During this period Sakharov began sending scientific articles to Moscow. Though none of these papers were published, the exercises helped shape his theories and boost his confidence as a scientist. Meanwhile, back in Moscow, his father had helped secure an invitation for Sakharov to attend the venerable Academy of Sciences, the most prestigious Soviet institute of its kind.

Acceptance at the academy was a fantastic opportunity for an up-and-coming physicist like Sakharov and presented him with the chance to practice theoretical physics at the pinnacle of his field. He would be a graduate student under the tutelage of Igor Tamm, the renowned Soviet physicist and future Nobel laureate. As it turned out, Sakharov was Tamm's star pupil. Over the years the two physicists would develop a close personal and professional relationship. Sakharov and Tamm would form the nucleus of the team that eventually designed the first hydrogen bomb.

While Sakharov was at the academy, the United States dropped the world's first atomic bombs on Nagasaki and Hiroshima, ending World War II. Sakharov learned about it on the morning of August 7, 1945, when he stopped to glance at a newspaper and discovered that a nuclear bomb of enormous destructive power had been dropped on Hiroshima. The news shocked him greatly.

Later he said:

> I was so stunned that my legs practically gave way. There could be no doubt that my fate and the fate of many others, perhaps of the entire world, had changed overnight. Something new and awesome had entered our lives, a product of the greatest of the sciences, of the discipline I revered.

He could not help but suspect that his work, and life, would be profoundly affected by this news.

Two years later, in 1947, Sakharov received his doctorate in physical and mathematical sciences. It was a formidable achievement for a person so young. In the Soviet Union the doctorate was usually awarded to older and more experienced scientists.

Sakharov continued to work under Tamm's guidance at the academy, studying relativity and quantum mechanics. There he was approached, in 1950, by Lavrenti Beria, Soviet leader Joseph Stalin's feared chief of police. Sakharov and Tamm were asked by Beria to join a top priority

"I was so stunned that my legs practically gave way. There could be no doubt that my fate and the fate of many others, perhaps of the entire world, had changed overnight. Something new and awesome had entered our lives, a product of the greatest of the sciences, of the discipline I revered."

or "crash" program already under way in a secret village in Turkmenia. The secret village was called the Installation. The project was to build the world's first hydrogen bomb. Before 1948 neither Sakharov nor Tamm was involved in any of the research that Soviet leader Joseph Stalin had established during the war. Sakharov's work in theoretical physics had led him into the field of thermonuclear reactions. By 1948, he had already published two seminal articles on the subject, earning quite a name for himself as a pioneer of scientific knowledge.

Beria was making an offer Sakharov found hard to refuse. It represented more than the greatest scientific challenge a physicist could expect to be offered. It was also a chance for Sakharov to contribute to his country's defenses. In the wake of World War II, which had devastated the Soviet Union, Sakharov believed his country needed nuclear weapons to ensure peace.

At the Soviet Union's top-secret Installation center, Sakharov would become one of a team of five scientists responsible for the development of the Soviet hydrogen bomb. His research, more than that of any other scientist, significantly altered the course of Soviet research on controlled thermonuclear reactions. After nearly three years of virtual isolation, the Installation team was ready to test the product of its effort. On August 12, 1953, a nuclear device was placed atop a tower and detonated.

Sakharov viewed the explosion from 20 miles away. With cold scientific detachment, he observed the formation of the mushroom cloud. Then, he dove to the ground as the shock wave rolled over them. Later he recalled how the explosion "blasted my ears and struck a sharp blow to my entire body," and how the mushroom cloud, "which now filled half the sky, turned a sinister blue-black color," before drifting south.

In the wake of his success, Sakharov, still only 32, was unanimously elected to the Academy of Science with a full membership—unheard of for someone so young. He and Tamm were awarded cash prizes of 500,000 rubles each, and each was given the Hero of Socialist Labor medal, the first of two that Sakharov would win.

At this time, celebrity status was rare for anyone behind the Iron Curtain. Sakharov was the young exception. He was now considered the Soviet Union's most prized possession, his genius a glittering national asset. He was considered the irrefutable proof of the superiority of the Communist system that had produced him.

After the hydrogen bomb test, Tamm returned to the academy. But Sakharov stayed at the Installation for 15 more years. There he conducted further research and enjoyed the prestige and orderly life of the top-secret laboratory. In these years he viewed the Soviet atomic program as a patriotic undertaking and a necessary deterrent to the growing nuclear arsenal of the United States.

Some of that research, however, would not be well received by the Soviet authorities, since it implied criticism of the Soviet nuclear program. Gradually Sakharov began to take a critical view of atomic tests, recognizing that they caused biological damage from radiation fallout. In a 1958 article published in the Soviet journal *Atomic Energy*, Sakharov suggested that the destructive power of a thermonuclear device was not the only threat posed by these weapons. He pointed out that the fallout alone from atmospheric tests would cause a huge number of victims, as the cancer-causing radiation drifted downwind.

Worried by the potential effects of radiation fallout that could result from a series of planned tests, Sakharov sent a letter of protest to Soviet headquarters at the Kremlin, citing statistics on genetic damage evident from previous tests. He reminded the Soviet authorities that these tests only served to increase international tension, thereby increasing the risk of nuclear holocaust. He even telephoned President Khrushchev, who vacillated, but remained unconvinced. "I would be a slob if I listened to the likes of Sakharov," he said. So the tests went ahead on schedule.

By this time Sakharov realized he was in a situation over which he had little control but one for which he felt enormous responsibility. Sakharov's moral character seemed to place him above politics, but his truth-telling nature created problems for government officials, and thrust him headlong into the political arena. Although Sakharov regarded his own courage and wisdom as nothing out of the ordinary, these qualities were not encouraged in Soviet scientists.

With the signing of the Nuclear Test Ban Treaty of 1963, Sakharov could rest a little easier. The treaty banned thermonuclear testing in the atmosphere, oceans, and outer space, a step Sakharov estimated would save hundreds of thousands of lives. By repeatedly voicing his concerns to top officials about the human dangers of these tests, Sakharov believed he had laid the groundwork for the Soviet Union's agreement to the treaty.

In the early 1960s, Sakharov took part in a public controversy involving the followers of Trofim D. Lysenko, a Soviet agronomist who maintained that acquired genetic characteristics could be transmitted to succeeding generations. Applying this theory to agriculture, Lysenko and his adherents tendered the promise of magnificent increases in crop production. Although Lysenko's theory had been largely discredited after Stalin's death, it had been revived by Khrushchev, who was seeking answers to the Soviet Union's long-standing problems with agriculture. Sakharov saw the theory as pseudoscience, while Khrushchev believed it held the promise of an extraordinary abundance of farm crops and animals. Despite warnings from Khrushchev, Sakharov refused to accept a theory that violated both the tenets of genetics and his integrity as a scientist. Sakharov was the first to speak out against Lysenko's theory, and the respect he had earned among his colleagues helped to break Lysenko's hold over Soviet science. He also helped free the scientific community from even greater political control.

Khrushchev was deposed in 1964, and Leonid Brezhnev came to power. In the years that followed there was an attempt to restore a degree of the Stalinist repression that Khrushchev had condemned. Suddenly it was easier to send political dissidents to the labor camps—the *gulags* of Siberia and other remote areas. In response, Sakharov and 24 other well-known personalities sent a letter of protest to President Brezhnev denouncing these actions. They warned that the Soviet people would neither accept nor understand any restoration of Stalin's brutal legacy. The letter was met with cold silence.

While Sakharov still held top-security clearances, he participated in many such "declarations." Rarely did he receive an official response, but he forged on, calling attention to public issues. As a blossoming and determined advocate of human rights, he saw public appeals as the only weapon at his disposal in his fight against human rights violations. At first the Kremlin listened to Sakharov's concerns with consideration and a degree of respect. Later, government officials began to treat him as an eccentric.

Restrictions on freedom of thought in the Soviet Union and the Soviet bloc countries reached their height in 1968, with open rebellion in Czechoslovakia during a period known as the Prague Spring. (In the Soviet Union, the "Prague Spring" became a catchphrase for the liberalization of Soviet life.) As a scientist, Sakharov considered freedom of thought as the one ingredient critical to any progress-based science, and to all efforts to solve the Soviet Union's problems.

Sakharov was deeply disappointed when the Soviet Union cracked down in Czechoslovakia, making it clear that there would be no tolerance of free expression anywhere in the Soviet empire. Simultaneously, he felt a growing compulsion to speak out on the fundamental issues of his time. Sakharov was compelled by the sense of personal responsibility he felt for his role in building the hydrogen bomb, and by his knowledge of the horrors of thermonuclear warfare.

Eventually he expressed these thoughts in a 10,000-word manuscript he wrote. In it Sakharov reflected on such global subjects as war, hunger, environmental pollution, and the stultifying qualities of mass culture. He also discussed the dangers of racism and nationalism, as well as the Stalinist and Maoist cults.

Sakharov's basic theses were that "the division of mankind threatens society with destruction" and that "intellectual freedom is essential to human society." He saw among the chief dangers facing humanity the perpetuation of "intellectually simplified, narrow-minded mass myths." Myths, he said, made nations prey to hysteria and the dogmatism of "cruel and treacherous demagogues."

The essay began to circulate clandestinely among the Soviet intelligentsia. Before long a copy found its way into the hands of a foreign journalist. In July of 1968 it was printed in its entirety by the *New York Times*, under the title *Progress, Coexistence and Intellectual Freedom*. In the West, observers were overjoyed that such humanitarian principles had managed to survive behind the Iron Curtain of Soviet repression. Eighteen million copies were printed worldwide.

> "The division of mankind threatens society with destruction."

When Soviet citizens heard the essay being read over the Voice of America, a radio station that broadcasts programming behind the Iron Curtain, the reaction from the Kremlin was predictable. Soviet authorities demanded that Sakharov publicly renounce the essay as a fraud. Sakharov refused. In consequence, he was removed from secret defense work and transferred back to the academy.

At the academy he was not expected to do much work. Instead, for the next 10 years, he devoted nearly all his time to the struggle against Soviet repression. In 1970 he helped form the Human Rights Committee, whose mission was to study and publicize human rights violations in the U.S.S.R. The committee was soon flooded with requests for help from individuals everywhere.

Sakharov's life had by now changed completely from his days of scientific work at the Installation. No longer was he practicing science at the frontiers of knowledge, and no longer was he seen as a national hero. His wife Klava had died of cancer in 1969, and his children did not understand their father's newfound mission and became estranged.

Through his work on the committee, Sakharov met Elena Bonner. She was a physician and a tireless advocate of human rights. Bonner's mother had spent years in Soviet prisons. Elena and Sakharov grew very close, and together they worked ceaselessly for the cause. Several times they staged hunger strikes together, in cases when they felt they had no other option in what often seemed a futile struggle against the state.

The couple was married in 1972, cementing their alliance. When Sakharov was awarded the Nobel Peace Prize in 1975 for his persistent defenses of human rights, Bonner traveled to Oslo to accept the honor because the government had denied her husband an exit visa. In delivering her husband's acceptance speech,

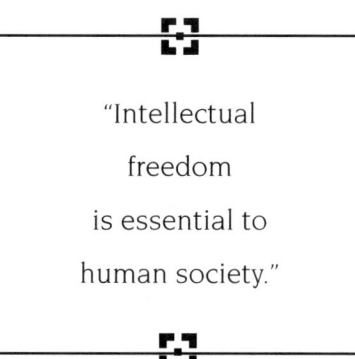

"Intellectual freedom is essential to human society."

Nobel Prize laureate Andrei Sakharov, with wife Elena, was an international human rights hero in the Soviet Union. (UPP/Photoreporters, Inc.)

she stressed the "urgency of intellectual freedom" and the necessity of governments and peoples everywhere to "make good the demands of reason." In the speech Sakharov added that he shared the award with prisoners of conscience everywhere who had sacrificed their own liberty in defending that of others.

The Norwegian Nobel Report declared that Dr. Sakharov "has fought not only against the abuse of power and violation of human dignity in all its forms, but has with equal vigor fought for the ideal of a state founded on the principle of justice." The report expressed the West's support for Sakharov for taking a bold stance for freedom while living under a totalitarian regime. The Soviet newspapers responded that Sakharov was "a laboratory rat of the West" for demonizing the Soviet Union.

Early in 1980, Sakharov spoke out against the Soviet presence in Afghanistan, asking the United States to pressure the Soviet Union to withdraw. For Soviet authorities this was the last straw. The government's tolerance had come to an end. While driving home from a grocery store on January 22, 1980, his car was pulled over by a policeman and escorted to the Procurator's Office. On the same day he was evicted from his Moscow home and exiled to Gorki, a closed military city 250 miles to the east.

Sakharov's "crime" was denouncing the Soviet invasion of Afghanistan. He saw the invasion as a simple product of Soviet expansionism, one that would bring about the needless pain and suffering of war. Bonner was notified and given two hours to pack, should she choose to accompany her husband. By 6 P.M. the Sakharovs were hustled aboard a plane bound for Gorki, a city off-limits to foreigners. He was stripped of all his privileges, medals, and titles.

In Gorki, the Sakharovs' mail was censored. Their apartment was kept under constant surveillance. There was no telephone access. Several times their apartment was broken into, and manuscripts, diaries, and even writings on scientific matters were confiscated. There was never any doubt that this was the work of the KGB, the Soviet secret police. Sakharov suspected that his landlady was involved in facilitating the breakins. Many completed chapters of his memoirs had to be rewritten several times because of these thefts, and Sakharov was forced to bring all of his important papers with him whenever he left the apartment.

While he was in Gorki, only Sakharov's family was allowed to see him. For entertainment, sometimes he and his wife would take a walk around the town, or go to the local movie theater. There was always the possibility that he could be allowed to return to Moscow, but only if he promised not to speak critically of the government. For Sakharov, this was unthinkable.

When foreign scientists came to the U.S.S.R. and asked about the brilliant scientist, academy officials told them that Dr. Sakharov was living in a beautiful apartment, with special food, a personal secretary, and excellent medical care. In fact, during the seven years Sakharov spent in exile, eight months were spent involuntarily in the hospital. There he suffered the indignity of forced feeding. This was the government's response to several of his hunger strikes. Once he was even released on the discovery that he had a cardiac condition. Apparently the Soviet authorities felt that a natural death would provide an easy solution to the public relations problems Sakharov had caused.

Despite being denounced and isolated in Gorki, with Bonner's help Sakharov continued his campaign against Soviet repression. He possessed the strength of character to resist repression long after the government had stripped him of his honors and privileges. Together, from their apartment, he and Bonner continued to send letters to heads of state and make numerous appeals to Soviet leaders, requesting the release of prisoners of conscience.

Bonner was his constant companion. She typed all her husband's correspondence and served as a lifeline to the outside world, delivering his mail and communicating on his behalf with family and friends. For this help Sakharov credited her with preserving not only his work, but also his dignity. It was common for her to be followed, detained, and searched during her trips between Gorki and Moscow. Moreover, the Soviet press kept up a full-scale campaign of vilification against her, painting her as the conniving woman who had corrupted the famous Russian scientist.

On May 20, 1984, Sakharov managed to get a letter to American diplomats in which he asked that his wife be given asylum in the U.S. embassy. He also urged that she be allowed to travel to the United States for medical treatment because of a heart condition. The response from Moscow was to threaten to arrest Bonner for what Soviet officials called her "anti-Soviet activities." She was not allowed to go to the United States.

At the end of 1986, change was in the air in the Soviet Union. Reformist Party leader Mikhail Gorbachev was showing signs of easing up on political dissidents. On December 15, government agents installed a telephone in the Sakharovs' apartment. The next day Sakharov received a phone call from Gorbachev informing him that he could return to Moscow and resume his scientific work. Gorbachev wanted Sakharov to lend credibility and support to his new policy of liberalization, known as *perestroika*.

A week later, on the morning of December 23, 1986, Sakharov and Bonner returned to Moscow. At the train station, they were surrounded by Soviet and foreign reporters and photographers. It was a crazy and hectic scene, with the 65-year-old physicist attempting to answer the deluge of questions amid blinding flashbulbs. It took Sakharov and his wife nearly an hour to escape the throng. Sakharov then attended a scientific seminar at the academy where his research had once been applauded by the scientific community. He told them he would continue to work for human rights.

Sakharov's release was a landmark event in the gradual democratization of the Soviet Union that continues to this day. In an attempt to legitimize the principle of formal opposition, the New Congress of the People's Deputies was established. This was a legislative body created to rebuild the nation, and in 1987 Sakharov won a seat on it easily.

Members of the Congress would be eligible for a seat on the Supreme Soviet—the most powerful legislative body in the nation. During his years as a deputy, Sakharov never ceased his call for the freedom of conscience that he maintained was a fundamental pillar of a humane society. Nor did he relent in his criticisms of Gorbachev. Sakharov felt that Gorbachev's policies of *glasnost* (freedom of speech) and *perestroika* were moving too slowly. With so many innocent people still serving sentences in Soviet prisons and labor camps, the famous scientist could not hide his impatience.

On December 14, 1989, at the age of 68, Sakharov suffered a stroke and died in his Moscow apartment. It was just three years since his release from Gorki. His funeral, on a gray, wet Moscow morning, was attended by thousands. Even Gorbachev appeared briefly to pay his respects to this genuine Russian hero.

In 1968 Harrison E. Salisbury, the *New York Times* reporter who had covered Sakharov more thoroughly than anyone else, compared Sakharov to the three scientists who led the Americans in developing the atomic and hydrogen bombs. He was, said Salisbury, "Oppenheimer, Teller, and Hans Bethe all rolled into one." This was a tribute to Sakharov's accomplishment in extending the borders of theoretical physics, and a compliment to his honest nationalism and rounded moral vision.

Soviet dissident Andrei Sakharov casts his vote in Moscow in March 1989 in an effort to defeat old guard candidates and force a second election. (AP/Wide World Photos)

Toward the end of his life Sakharov was dismayed to learn that he had come to be regarded by many as a hero. His vision was of a society without heroes. He recognized freedom as something achieved and sustained by ordinary individuals, with everyone taking an active role. He will long be remembered by citizens of the Soviet Union for his own selfless struggle against tyranny, and as a beacon of freedom to citizens of the world everywhere.

Chronology

May 21, 1921	Born outside of Moscow
1938	Graduates from high school with honors
1941	Relocated to Ashkabad during World War II
1942	Graduates from Moscow State University
July 10, 1942	Marries Klava Vikhireva
1942–45	Works at munitions factory on the Volga River
1945	Enrolls as a graduate student at Lebedev Physical Institute at the Soviet Academy of Sciences
1950	Recruited to work at the Installation
August 12, 1953	Demonstrates thermonuclear explosion
1968	Publishes *Reflections on Progress, Coexistence and Intellectual Freedom*
March 8, 1969	Wife Klava dies of stomach cancer
1969	Transferred back to the Academy of Sciences
1972	Marries Elena Bonner
1975	Awarded the Nobel Peace Prize
January 22, 1980	Exiled to closed military city of Gorki

1986	Freed by Gorbachev
1987	Elected to the Congress of People's Deputies
December 14, 1989	Dies in his Moscow apartment

Further Reading

Babyonyshev, Alexander, ed. *On Sakharov.* New York: Knopf, 1982. Translated essays by various Soviet writers and scientists honoring Sakharov's 60th birthday.

Bailey, George. *Galileo's Children: Science, Sakharov, and the Power of the State.* New York: Arcade Publishing, 1990. An absorbing account of history, politics, and the role of the state in the development of science.

LaVert, Suzanne. *The Sakharov File: A Study in Courage.* New York: Messner, 1986. Recounts the lives of Sakharov and his wife against a background of Russian history.

Sakharov, Andrei. *Memoirs.* New York: Arcade Publishing, 1990. The dissident's own detailed personal account of his life and work.

Alexander Dubcek as chairman of the Federal Assembly, a post he held briefly. (UPP/Photoreporters, Inc.)

Alexander Dubcek

"An old wise man said, 'If there once was light, why should there be darkness again?' Let us act in such a way as to bring the light back again." When Alexander Dubcek spoke those words to hundreds of thousands of his fellow citizens in 1989, he hadn't made a public pronouncement in 20 years. Now, in the midst of Czechoslovakia's peaceful Velvet Revolution, he found that he was still a hero among those who remembered his bold attempts at reform 20 years earlier, and how he was forced into internal exile.

During the first eight months of 1968, a period known as the Prague Spring, Dubcek had tried to create what he termed "a free, modern, and profoundly humane society" as first secretary of the Czechoslovak Communist Party. He had wanted to give socialism a "human face," but when the armed forces of the Soviet Union and its Warsaw Pact allies invaded Czechoslovakia, he was stripped of his authority and tossed out of the Communist Party.

Until the Velvet Revolution, the Communist regime was based on a single lie—that the Soviet invasion of 1968 to crush Dubcek's liberal government had been a fraternal act of assistance for which all Czechs and Slovaks should be grateful. Historians, however, are convinced that the "freedom" the Czechoslovaks briefly enjoyed in 1968 was a prologue to the revolutions that

> took place 20 years later, not just in Czechoslovakia but in all of Eastern Europe. Thus, Dubcek was a reformer 20 years ahead of his time.

Alexander Dubcek was born in the small village of Uhrovec in the Strazovska Mountains of western Slovakia, on November 27, 1921, to Stefan and Pavlina Dubcek. His family was Slovak. The Slovaks were a people who had lived side by side with Czechs for centuries, but Dubcek's parents resented the oppressive Czech rulers. A decade before the birth of Alexander they had immigrated to the United States, hoping to improve their fortunes. But the young couple found America to be a huge disappointment. During World War I Dubcek's father was interned for 14 months in Texas because he refused to be drafted into the United States military. A few months before Alexander's birth, his parents, with their oldest child Julius, returned to their homeland, only to leave Slovakia a few years later for the Soviet Union.

Alexander was three years old when, on a rainy day in the spring of 1925, his father packed up the family again and moved to Kirghizia—now Kyrgyzstan—near the Chinese border in Soviet Central Asia. They moved there, along with a small colony of several hundred Czechs and Slovaks, in response to an appeal from Moscow for Czechoslovaks to come to the new Soviet Union and help build socialism there. The 30-day, 4,000-mile train ride was long and tiring. When the group finally arrived, they were sorely disappointed. Nobody was there to greet them, much less bring them to the modest houses they had been promised by Soviet officials. Eventually, the family found shelter in an abandoned army barracks.

With great determination, and possessing an unbending faith in the promising new ideology of communism, Alexander's father kept the family in Kirghizia for eight years. Alexander obtained his early education at local schools and attended secondary school at Frunze, the regional capital. In 1933 his family moved to Gorki, a city some 230 miles east of Moscow. There Alexander was finally enrolled in a proper school. He was a shy, studious boy who spoke Russian fluently and excelled in his other studies as well.

He adapted well to Gorki and was happy, yet all around him there was much unhappiness. He lived in the Soviet Union during some of that country's most turbulent years, the Red Terror of the 1930s. It was a time when Soviet leader Joseph Stalin was on a mission to rid the Communist Party of any potential threat to his leadership. Contact with foreigners, such as the Dubcek family, became dangerous for Soviet citizens. As loyal Communists, the Dubceks did not question Stalin's policies, nor were they harmed. But by 1938, the widespread killing and deportations convinced them that it would be best to leave the Soviet Union.

The family returned to Slovakia in 1938, one year before Nazi Germany violated the Munich Agreement and marched into Czechoslovakia. Alexander had begun to work at odd jobs—as a chauffeur, as a gas station attendant, and as a page boy at a local hotel—when the Germans set up an "independent" state of Slovakia, under German "protection." Though still only a teenager, he lost little time in rallying to the anti-Nazi cause. He joined the new Slovak Communist Party, illegal under the Slovak puppet regime controlled by Germany's Adolf Hitler, a staunch anti-Communist.

It was in this newly created Slovak party that Dubcek met many of the men who would be his comrades-in-arms. Soon after, he went to work as a locksmith in one of the Skoda armaments factories close to the Slovak town of Trencin, where the Dubcek family had settled. Dubcek, as part of a small, tightly knit Communist cell in his factory, was assigned to the job of foiling the Germans by sabotaging production and stealing as much equipment as possible from the armaments factory. It was a small-scale, but nevertheless very dangerous, clandestine activity that could easily have cost him his life.

Both Alexander and his older brother Julius also helped train Slovak platoons (party members) for guerrilla warfare—harassing the Germans wherever they could in the lower Tatra Mountains of Slovakia. In the summer of 1944, Alexander and Julius led a full-scale revolt that was swiftly put down by the Nazis. Extra forces from Germany's secret police, the Gestapo, flooded Slovakia. Julius was killed and Alexander was shot twice in the thigh. He had to be carried on a stretcher to a local house. There he was nursed back to health by a local Slovak woman, Anna Ondrisova. In the fall of 1945, Dubeck and Anna were married.

After World War II, Dubcek got a job as a laborer in a yeast factory in Trencin and became more involved in party work. He was only 24 years old. Nevertheless, he was not too young to be appointed party secretary at his factory. His duties for this unpaid job, which he performed in his spare time, included recruiting new members, organizing meetings, and collecting dues.

In 1949, one year after elections swept Communists to victory in Czechoslovakia, Dubcek left his job at the yeast factory to become a part of the Communist bureaucracy. It was his first important political post—secretary of the Trencin district committee of the Communist Party. Soon he began moving up the Communist Party ladder. In 1951 he became a member of the central committee of the Slovak Communist Party in Bratislava, the region's capital. Bratislava, a centuries-old city on the Danube River, was also the third-largest city in Czechoslovakia. There Dubcek was also elected to the Legislative Assembly.

By 1951 he was a full-time, if minor, party functionary. Part of his job was to pass on party directives from Prague to the smaller regions and districts, so he was always well informed about inside developments. But, as he had in the

Soviet Union, Dubcek was usually inclined to believe what the party said. After Stalin's death, the reshuffling of power in the Kremlin was quickly followed by a similar reshuffling in Prague. Dubcek was promoted.

He became regional party secretary of Banska Bystrica, a town framed by the mountains in central Slovakia. Dubcek was pleased that this new job would bring him into contact with ordinary people again. He was responsible for developing economic resources and implementing government policies. For two years, he presided over the partial industrialization of the town's economy. During his tenure, four large new factories were built: a lumber mill, a textile factory, a pharmaceutical laboratory, and a cement works.

Now the father of three young sons—Peter, Pavel, and Milan—Dubcek was a committed family man who spent his free time with his children, his wife or his parents. On weekends he worked in the garden or took his sons to soccer games. The family frequently enjoyed hiking together in the forest or swimming at the municipal swimming pool. Unlike so many of his colleagues, Dubcek enjoyed a simple life. He shunned the special vacation resorts reserved for high party officials.

While at Banska Bystrica, Dubcek began to study law at night, and he was eventually awarded a degree from Comenius University in Bratislava. Then, in 1955, he was sent by the Slovak Communist Party to Moscow's prestigious Higher Party School to study political science, mostly Marxist-Leninist philosophy, for three years.

In Moscow he learned a great deal about politics from watching the dramatic denunciation of Stalin by the new Soviet leader, Nikita Khrushchev. Dubcek also came to the attention of Antonin Novotny, the first secretary of Czechoslovakia's Communist Party. Novotny was impressed by the young apparatchik, or Communist Party functionary. Reportedly, he told Dubcek's father: "I predict that he will go far in the party."

Novotny was right. Dubcek returned to Czechoslovakia with newly acquired political savvy that carried him up through the ranks of the Communist Party. Dubcek was made chief secretary of the regional committee of the Communist Party of Slovakia in Bratislava. At the 1960 national conference of the Communist Party of Czechoslovakia, he was elected to the central committees of both the regional Slovak and the national Czechoslovak Communist parties.

That same year, he made his first move from the regional to the national political arena. He was named to the secretariat of the Central Committee of the Czechoslovak Communist Party in Prague. In this position, Dubcek handled issues relating to industrial policy, and witnessed the decline of Czechoslovakia's industry. But, like his father, Dubcek blamed human failings, rather than the centralized economic system, for the predicament. He still believed that if only people would work harder, then the economy could revive.

In 1963 Dubcek was named first secretary of the Slovak Communist Party, the most important job in Slovakia. Even though he was the highest-ranking Communist in Slovakia, he walked to work every morning from his Bratislava home, foregoing the chauffeured limousine that was available to him. Meanwhile, he was undergoing a major change in his thinking. Gradually he began to view the inefficient economic system with skepticism. He started to see that if the party made mistakes, then the party needed to take responsibility for them.

Dubcek was certainly not alone in this view. In 1967, he would lead like-minded Communists in confronting the corrupt party directly. In late October, at a meeting of the party's Central Committee in Prague, Dubcek criticized First Party Secretary Antonin Novotny for his abuse of power. By January 5, Novotny was forced to step down. That same day, Dubcek was named first party secretary of the Czechoslovak Communist Party.

Most Czechoslovaks knew little about Dubcek when he came to power. Though more than six feet tall, the 46-year-old Dubcek did not cut a very striking figure. He wore ill-fitting suits and was regarded as somewhat shy and nervous, certainly not one given to impulsive action. As a loyal Communist with strong party credentials, he was popular both in and out of the party. Yet this new leader seemed different from other high-ranking officials. In his humbleness and compassion he contrasted sharply with the faceless party bureaucrats the Czechoslovaks had grown used to. When he got Novotny's job, for instance, Dubcek kept his family's modest five-room house in Bratislava. He took a room in the party hotel in Prague and commuted home on weekends.

Dubcek believed he could reform the Communist Party from within and promote "democratization" in Czechoslovakia. Within weeks of taking office, he stunned Moscow and the rest of the world with his publicly stated determination to achieve the "widest possible democratization" of Czechoslovakia. Immediately he began to relax the party's censorship of Czechoslovak newspapers and broadcasts. He permitted the Writers' Union, a group of militant dissidents, to write freely and to edit a literary journal. He sent out word that the political vendettas of the past were over.

As his first real order of business, Dubcek sought to learn as much as possible about the real state of affairs in Czechoslovakia. For the first three weeks of January 1968, he read scores of reports. When he gained access to the confidential archives for the first time, he was horrified by what he learned.

To revive the economy, Dubcek called on many intellectuals for ideas. They provided him with the theoretical underpinnings and factual analysis on which to fashion a truly ambitious reform program. By early February he gave the first public intimations of what was to come. In a speech to 1,800 delegates at the Seventh Congress of Unified Agricultural

Cooperatives, Dubcek called on the country's farmers to help shape their own future:

> Democracy is not only the right and chance to pronounce one's own views, but also the way in which the people's views are handled. Government organs must strive to create the optimum conditions in which farmers can apply their skills and initiative, not to give orders on when and how to reap and sow.

On April 10, 1968, Dubcek published a 52-page document called the Action Program. The program, introduced as official party policy, was a dramatic break from the past. Dubcek's radical document called for the right of all citizens to free expression and free assembly. He promised to guarantee these rights by amendments to the constitution and called for non-Communist parties to participate in political life.

What Dubcek published was truly revolutionary. He said that censorship was to be curtailed. He advocated the right to travel, even to live abroad. He granted the right to seek restitution from the government's illegal seizure of property, and he restructured the economy to guarantee the emergence of a market. Businesses were to be granted far greater independence from government control. Even trade with Western capitalist countries was to be expanded.

It was a radical departure from the traditional party line, under which

> "Democracy is not only the right and chance to pronounce one's own views, but also the way in which the people's views are handled. Government organs must strive to create the optimum conditions in which farmers can apply their skills and initiative, not to give orders on when and how to reap and sow."

the party had controlled all decision-making authority in practically every sphere of life. Now open forums sprang up all over the country. In villages and town halls, at schools and universities, in factories and offices, people began to express what they really thought. Censorship ended and journalists began to write and broadcast reports that addressed the most controversial issues of the day.

In the spring of 1968, Dubcek was everyone's man of the hour in Czechoslovakia. On May Day, the holiday honoring the workers of the world, Czechoslovaks turned out in droves to celebrate. Whereas in the past Czechoslovaks had to be "persuaded" to attend the festivities held each year, they now celebrated wildly in the streets. Dubcek mingled with the crowds. A man of the people, he was photographed cheering for his favorite soccer team in Bratislava and signing his autograph for dozens of waiting children. He made a point of talking to people on the street, taking notes on their comments and problems.

Dubcek's accessibility and lack of pretension won over the Czechoslovak people. When he announced that gold reserves in Czechoslovakia were low, thousands of women demonstrated their support by donating their gold wedding bands to the government. Dubcek's picture appeared on the cover of *Time* magazine. Reporters followed his every move, filing stories every week about the enormous popularity he enjoyed.

This popularity was heady wine in 1968. Nothing remotely resembling such independence had existed in Eastern Europe since the Hungarian uprising of 1956, which had been crushed by Soviet troops. Though Dubcek did not always initiate these changes, none of them could have come about without his blessing. Party conformists inside and outside Czechoslovakia were amazed and angry at the steps Dubcek was taking to loosen the stringent control of the Soviet Union.

Dubcek quickly found himself at odds with both the Kremlin and more radical reformers eager for speedier reforms. Between these two extremes he tried to steer a middle course. Dubcek could not understand how democratic-minded reformers could be impatient with what was already a blistering pace of change. He knew that he could move only so fast on reform without provoking a strong reaction from the Soviet Union. On several occasions, he seemed to be trying to reassure the Soviets by publicly warning that "the enemies of socialism" would not be tolerated.

More than anything else, Dubcek felt the long shadow of the crackdown in Hungary 12 years earlier. Dubcek was right to fear a Soviet invasion. The move that most frightened Soviet leader Leonid Brezhnev and Czechoslovakia's neighboring Communist leaders was Dubcek's call for non-Communists to be allowed to participate in government. To the other Communist leaders, ending the party's monopoly on power meant sharing power with others—and eventually giving it up completely.

To Brezhnev, the events in Czechoslovakia smacked of counterrevolution, and he made his displeasure known. Dubcek was called to face Brezhnev and the other four Soviet bloc leaders several times between March and August of 1968. Upon returning to Prague, Dubcek did not censor the press but simply implored journalists not to antagonize the Soviet Union. As he told a friend, "I just try to smile at Brezhnev as he shouts at me. I say yes, yes. I agree and then I come home and do nothing."

Ominously, the Soviets announced in May that they planned to conduct "routine" military maneuvers on Czechoslovak and Polish soil. Dubcek could not refuse. Throughout June, the nervous Czechoslovaks continued their reforms while Soviet tanks rumbled through Czechoslovakia's countryside. In July of 1968 Brezhnev sent Dubcek a letter demanding that he come to Warsaw and halt the reforms immediately. Dubcek politely refused.

Brezhnev then wrote a stinging message that came to be known as the Warsaw Letter. The Soviet leader called the Czechoslovak reforms a betrayal of socialism and the Communist Party. He warned Dubcek that the Soviet Union was prepared to act. By mid-July, Communist leaders from East Germany, Hungary, and Bulgaria began deliberating in Warsaw over what had become known as the "Dubcek problem." Conspicuously absent from the meeting was Dubcek himself. He would have nothing to do with the gathering, which he saw as meddling in the internal affairs of a sovereign nation.

At that point, the relationship between Moscow and Prague crumbled rapidly. In July 1968, the Soviet authorities reluctantly agreed to a meeting between Dubcek and Brezhnev on Czechoslovak soil near the Soviet border. For four days, Brezhnev raged at Dubcek for hours at a time. Dubcek had publicly promised the Czechoslovak people that he would not cave in to Soviet pressure. He resisted Brezhnev's insistence that the important liberal reforms of the Prague Spring be rescinded.

The result was a stalemate, with neither side conceding anything. When he returned to Prague, Dubcek believed he had averted disaster one more time. In the weeks that followed, the reformist Czechoslovak leader got some words of encouragement from President Tito of Yugoslavia and President Nicolae Ceausescu of Romania.

In any case, Dubcek's luck had finally run out. At 10:30 P.M. on August 20, 1968, a fleet of Soviet warplanes landed at Prague's Ruzyne Airport. Soon the sky was filled with planes. On cue, men waiting in the airport lounge drew revolvers and burst into the control room. The Soviet invasion of Czechoslovakia had begun. By morning, Czechoslovakia was once again an occupied country. The hope that had been the Prague Spring ended abruptly.

Before the night was over, more than 200,000 troops from the five Warsaw Pact countries—the Soviet Union, Bulgaria, East Germany, Poland, and Hungary—had crossed the Czechoslovak border at 18 different points. They would be joined by an additional 300,000 troops the following week. At the peak of the invasion in late August, there would be some 650,000 Warsaw Pact soldiers in Czechoslovakia.

For days the world read accounts of the invasion and watched it on television. They saw thousands of unarmed Czechoslovak students and workers confronting Soviet tanks and soldiers with flowers and placards, pleading with them to go home. The crowd tore down street signs, replacing them with signs reading "Dubcek Boulevard" so that foreign soldiers, relying on maps, would lose their way around the cities, towns, and villages.

Spontaneous demonstrations occurred. Sporadic violence erupted as crowds hurled insults at the troops. Within a few days, 20 Czechoslovaks had been killed and more than 300 were wounded in Prague. In the first week alone, at least 186 people were killed and more than 360 were seriously wounded.

As Soviet tanks rumbled through the streets of Prague, the Czechoslovak Communist Party held its 14th Party Congress in secret and reelected Dubcek first secretary. In the morning several Soviet military vehicles pulled up outside the Central Committee building. Dubcek and a handful of other officials were arrested and flown to the Soviet Union, where they were imprisoned in Moscow. In the immediate aftermath of the invasion, no one knew whether he was dead or alive.

On August 23, a number of remaining high-ranking Czechoslovak officials were flown to Moscow to negotiate the release of Dubcek and the others. The delegation told the Soviets that the people of Czechoslovakia were united in their resistance to the invasion. Brezhnev accepted the fact that he had to allow Dubcek to stay on for a while as Czechoslovakia's leader. When Dubcek returned on August 26, five days after the invasion, his Prague Spring was finished. In Moscow, under pressure from the Soviets, he had agreed to enforce tighter controls within Czechoslovakia and to cut back on trade with the West.

A few days later, back in Prague, Dubcek choked back tears as he begged his people to continue to trust him. The sad-faced Czechoslovak leader told his people that he hoped to preserve as many of the reforms as possible, although "we might be forced to take some temporary measures that limit democracy and freedom of opinion." In truth, he could promise nothing. Still, he urged an end to the confrontation and asked his people for self-control. The emotional speech was broadcast to the entire nation.

Back in office, he gradually lost power while hard-line puppets of the Soviet regime reasserted themselves. Finally, on April 17, 1969, Dubcek was replaced by Gustav Husak as first secretary of the Czechoslovak Communist Party. Once a radical reformer, Husak had softened his positions and had made numerous concessions to the Soviets. Later that month, Dubcek was named chairman of the Czechoslovakian parliament, called Federal Assembly.

He was in that post on August 20, 1969, the first anniversary of the Soviet invasion. To commemorate the event, crowds gathered spontaneously in Prague's Wenceslas Square, shouting "Long Live Dubcek!" The police moved in to put down the demonstration. Half a dozen people were killed, and some 1,400 were arrested. This was the pretext used by the government to impose emergency laws suspending civil liberties. In a bitter irony, as chairman of the Federal Assembly, Dubcek had to sign those laws into effect.

It was clear that the Soviet plan was to ease Dubcek out slowly. In October 1969, he was relieved of his Federal Assembly position and dispatched to Turkey, where he served as Czechoslovak ambassador to Ankara. It was rumored that the leadership hoped Dubcek would use the opportunity to defect to the West, but he did not. Instead, he was a virtual prisoner in his own embassy for the six months he was ambassador. The same was true for Anna Dubcek. The couple's every move was monitored and controlled by the Soviet embassy in Ankara. Their three sons had remained with relatives in Czechoslovakia.

On May 25, 1970, Dubcek was thrown out of the Communist Party altogether and recalled to Prague. On Prague Radio, Dubcek was called "a renegade, traitor, revisionist, and failure." The following month he was banished to an even more obscure job dealing with forestry in his native Bratislava. He remained there, working as a mechanic for the Forestry Department, until 1987.

After he was expelled from the Communist Party, Dubcek's name was never mentioned in official media except to be vilified. His image was airbrushed out of the official photographs. Although technically free, Dubcek was constantly watched and followed by the security police. Former associates were warned not to visit him. From then on Dubcek would socialize only with his family and very close friends. He had vanished altogether from the world stage, and he refused to be interviewed by journalists.

At his villa outside Bratislava, the former Communist Party leader had turned to gardening in his spare time. But then, following a visit to Czechoslovakia in 1987 by the new reform-minded Soviet leader, Mikhail Gorbachev, Dubcek's police guards were removed. Slowly he began to emerge from isolation by speaking out through journalists. In 1988 he traveled to Italy, his first trip abroad in 20 years, to receive an honorary degree from Bologna University.

Later he appeared on Hungarian television accusing the Communist Party chief Milos Jakes of "treachery." In November 1989 he delivered a speech before a huge rally in Bratislava, as the wave of nationwide strikes and demonstrations that would sweep communism from power reached its crest. Dubcek, a relic from the past, announced that he still sided with the forces of reform. He said he backed Vaclav Havel, the playwright who had been jailed by the Communists, and his 1989 Velvet Revolution.

The erosion of the leadership of the Czechoslovak Communist regime in 1989 may have been speeded by news from Moscow. There Gorbachev had declared that rapid change in Eastern Europe was "necessary to make up for lost time." Dubcek was somewhat vindicated in November when the Soviet weekly *Moscow News* bitterly attacked the 1968 invasion of Czechoslovakia as "collective murder." Dubcek's Prague Spring had been "the first *perestroika* in the socialist countries," the magazine declared. "We crushed and slandered it."

After 20 years, things were heating up again. In November, 25,000 Czech students marched through Prague demanding democracy and free elections. Riot police moved in and attacked the students—but the attack only infuriated the Czechs. Three days later, more than 200,000 Czechs poured into Wenceslas Square. By the end of the week, half a million demonstrators turned out to chant and cheer.

On the morning of December 4, Dubcek stepped off the 9 A.M. bus from Bratislava into the cold Prague air. He made his way to the ongoing demonstrations in Wenceslas Square. Young protesters now knew the former leader only from yellowing photographs that had hung in Czechoslovak living rooms for two decades—pictures recalling the crushing of the Prague Spring movement. Dubcek was seen that night on national television for the first time since 1968. Instantly he began to gain the status of a shadow government leader.

"An old wise man said, 'If there once was light, why should there be darkness again?'"

At a rally the next day, his voice grew louder. Half a million singing and cheering Czechoslovaks braved the bitter cold and roared "Dubcek for president! Dubcek for president!" They wished him a "long life" and urged him to "take the castle"—a reference to the Communist seat of power. It had been a long journey across two decades, almost 21 years to the day since Dubcek had been removed from Prague in handcuffs. Just days before his 68th birthday, Dubcek was once again a Czechoslovakian national hero.

He looked out over the sea of cheering demonstrators. Dubcek called for democracy and freedom and urged Czechs to overthrow the Stalinist regime that still ruled them.

Scarcely an hour later, as he spoke at an opposition conference, Dubcek heard some astonishing news: Czechoslovakia's hard-line Communist Party chief, Milos Jakes, had just resigned, along with the country's entire ruling Politburo. Czechoslovakia finally had its revolution from below. For Dubcek it was a wonderful irony that his return coincided, almost to the moment, with Jakes's resignation.

Many were wondering if the Velvet Revolution, as it was known, would carry Dubcek back to power. Czechoslovakia's leading opposition figure, the playwright Vaclav Havel, was the clear choice for the presidency. At Havel's insistence, Dubcek became chairman of the Federal Parliament. In the end, the man whom time had not forgotten was unanimously elected speaker of Parliament, as Havel became president. Dubcek finally had his old job back, in the Federal Assembly.

On December 29, Dubcek stood in Hradcany Castle and proposed Havel's election to the presidency. That night, when he introduced the new president on the balcony overlooking Wenceslas Square, throngs of Czechoslovaks cheered him wildly.

Although he opposed the subsequent breakup of Czechoslovakia, Dubcek had been mentioned as a possible candidate to become president of an independent Slovakia. Dubcek maintained that the Prague Spring would have led to a pluralist, multiparty society much like the one Havel was creating. He once summed up the Prague Spring as the time when "we began to trust the people and the people began to trust us." As it turned out, the Prague Spring had been just the beginning of a new Czechoslovakia.

Dubcek said he was no longer a Communist in any sense, no longer even a Communist "with a human face." He said that he had never feared for his life, but that when he thought of all that had happened to the people of Czechoslovakia, "tears come to my eyes easily."

Tragically, on September 1, 1992, a car driven by Dubcek's chauffeur slid off a Prague highway in a rainstorm and plunged down a steep ravine. Dubcek suffered serious spine and chest injuries and underwent surgery. For several weeks he was in critical condition. Finally, he died of multiple organ failure on November 7, 1992.

Dubcek biographer William Shawcross agreed with a comment made by Soviet dissident Andrei Sakharov, who hailed Dubcek as a hero who gave Eastern Europe its first "breath of freedom" in 1968. "It had taken twenty-one more years for that breath to be turned into an irresistible gale," said Shawcross. "But it then swept away Stalinism."

Chronology

November 27, 1921	Born in the village of Uhrovec in the Strazovska Mountains of western Slovakia
Spring 1925	Moves with family to Kirghizia, in the Soviet Union
1933	Moves with family to Gorki, 235 miles east of Moscow
1938	Family returns to Slovakia; Dubcek joins Slovak Communist Party
Summer 1944	Wounded while leading revolt against Nazis
November 1945	Marries Anna Ondrisova

1949	Takes post as secretary of the party's Trencin district committee
1951	Becomes a member of the Central Committee in Bratislava
1953	Becomes regional party secretary of Banska Bystrica, in central Slovakia
1955	Sent to Moscow's prestigious Higher Party School for three years
1960	Elected to the central committees of both the regional Slovak and the national Czechoslovak Communist parties
1967	Takes on corrupt party officials
October 1967	Blasts First Party Secretary Antonin Novotny
January 5, 1968	Becomes first party secretary of the Communist Party
February 1968	Calls on farmers to help shape their own future
April 10, 1968	Publishes document calling for non-Communist parties to participate in political processes
May 1968	Soviets announce plan to hold Warsaw Pact military maneuvers on Czechoslovak soil
July 1968	Meets for four days with Brezhnev in Czechoslovakia. Refuses demands to halt reforms
August 20, 1968	Reforms of the Prague Spring end as more than 200,000 troops from the five Warsaw Pact countries begin invasion of Czechoslovakia
August 21, 1968	Arrested and flown to Moscow
August 26, 1968	Returns to Prague to say his reforms have been rescinded

April 17, 1969	Replaced as first secretary of the Communist party and later demoted to chairman of the Federal Assembly
October 1969	Relieved of his Federal Assembly position and sent to Turkey as Czechoslovak ambassador
May 25, 1970	Dismissed from the Communist Party and recalled to Prague
1988	Travels to Italy to receive an honorary degree from Bologna University
November 1989	Gives speech in Bratislava in which he supports dissident Vaclav Havel
December 4, 1989	Addresses crowd of protesters in an emotional speech on Wenceslas Square in Prague
December 1989	Named chairman of the Federal Parliament
November 7, 1992	Succumbs to multiple organ failure and dies following car accident in September

Further Reading

Dubcek, Alexander. *Hope Dies Last*. New York: Kodansha International, 1993. Dubcek's memoir, written in the wake of the Velvet Revolution, traces his life from his upbringing as a Communist ideologist through his return to public life 21 years after the Prague Spring.

Navazelskis, Ina. *Alexander Dubcek*. New York: Chelsea House, 1990. Follows the life of the Czechoslovakian leader from his transformation from Communist Party functionary to Prague Spring reformer, his banishment, and his comeback in the Velvet Revolution 20 years later.

Shawcross, William. *Dubcek*. New York: Simon & Schuster, 1990. The best biography of Dubcek, presented against the background of the Soviet invasion that ended the Prague Spring. Updated to include Dubcek's resurrection in the Velvet Revolution.

Boris Yeltsin, president of Russia. (UPP/Photoreporters, Inc.)

Boris Yeltsin

When he first emerged into prominence as Soviet leader Mikhail Gorbachev's chief critic, Boris Yeltsin was thought by many diplomats to be a crude and brutish operator who would be quickly swept aside by Gorbachev. Instead it happened the other way around. Gorbachev was deftly swept aside by Yeltsin, who emerged, surprisingly, as a man of rock-solid permanence during Russia's very delicate transition to democracy.

A supporter of *glasnost*, Gorbachev's policy of freedom of speech, and *perestroika*, a term for economic restructuring, Yeltsin had been demoted for wanting to take Gorbachev's policies too far, too fast. Although he was demoted and publicly admonished, Yeltsin refused to be silenced. Instead he thoroughly discredited Gorbachev. By the sheer force of his will and courage, he succeeded in making himself the first nationally and democratically elected leader in Russian history.

Boris Nikolayevish Yeltsin was born on February 1, 1931, in the village of Butko in Sverdlovsk Province, to Klavdia Vasilievna and Nikolai Ignatievich. The oldest of six children, he was born in a small house on a collective farm for peasants. It was a time of very bad harvests and hard times in Sverdlovsk, an industrial area of 1.2 million people in the Ural Mountains region of European Russia. Gangs of outlaws roamed at large. Shootouts, murders, and robberies were common occurrences.

In order to save the family, Yeltsin's father left the farm to find work on a construction site. This was during Stalin's so-called period of industrialization, when the Soviet Union was developing its heavy industry. Boris's father knew that construction workers would be needed for the building of a potash plant at Berezniki in the neighboring province of Perm, so he moved the family there and went to work as a laborer. While Boris's father labored at the building site, his mother, a gentle and kind woman, helped relatives and neighbors by sewing clothes.

Boris was five years old and had a younger brother and sister. The family lived in a crowded wooden hut typical of housing conditions of the time. There were no modern conveniences, only an outdoor toilet and water drawn from a well.

Young Boris made some money every summer at a nearby collective farm. In the hot sun he and his mother were allotted several acres of meadowland. They scythed the grass, stacked it, and prepared the hay—half of which went to the collective farm and half to the Yeltsins.

Boris attended several schools and showed early political ambitions. He was elected class leader each year, and earned top grades as a student. But along with academic abilities came a mischievous nature. In fifth grade, for instance, he persuaded his entire class to jump out the first-floor window. When the teacher returned, her classroom was empty.

Boris had a quick temper and a blunt way of speaking his mind. When he graduated from elementary school, Boris's outspokenness showed itself unmistakably. He waited until some 600 people had gathered for the graduation ceremony and then asked to make a speech. He thanked many of the school's teachers for their fine work. Then he began to openly criticize his homeroom teacher, accusing her of deliberately humiliating his fellow students and dampening their interest in learning. On and on he went with his blistering tirade until the graduation program was brought to a hasty conclusion.

The flabbergasted school board refused to give him his diploma, but Boris did not let the matter end there. He insisted that the government investigate the teacher's conduct—and before long she was dismissed.

On one occasion the consequences of his impulsiveness would scar him forever. During World War II, he and several chums had decided to break into a local church that was being used as an ammunitions depot. There Boris found several hand grenades. In a forest 40 miles away, he volunteered to take one of the grenades apart. Not realizing that he first had to remove the fuse, he put a grenade on a stone, knelt down and hit it with a hammer. The grenade exploded, mangling his left hand. He lost consciousness, and gangrene set in. When he came to, surgeons had removed two of his fingers.

In eighth grade he attended Sverdlovsk's Pushkin School, where he developed a lifelong passion for sports. He threw himself into volleyball, gymnastics, boxing, wrestling, and track. In the end, however, the young athlete settled on volleyball, playing it endlessly, in spite of the two-digit deficit on his left hand.

Gradually Boris began training to be a civil engineer. He entered the Department of Engineering at the Urals M. Kirov Polytechnic Institute. During his first year he plunged into extracurricular activities. He became president of the sports association, which meant organizing all sporting events. He was also captain of the city's volleyball team.

Within a year he was playing for the Sverdlovsk Senior League. During his five years at the institute, he traveled all over the Soviet Union, competing against the best volleyball teams in the country. It was after his first year that Boris caught the travel bug. That summer he decided to make a journey around the Soviet Union. Traveling alone, he hitched rides on trucks and passenger trains. Sometimes he rode on the roofs of trains, sometimes on the open platform at either end of the passenger cars. The hobo traveler slept in parks and train stations and returned home in rags after his two-month journey.

Boris was often away with the volleyball team, which left little time to spend with his sweetheart, Naya Girina. The couple had met and fallen deeply in love during their second year in school, but both kept very busy schedules. After graduation, Boris was assigned by the government to his home province of Sverdlovsk, while Naya was ordered to her home province of Orenburg. Ironically, a year's time apart cemented the relationship. When the couple reunited in 1956, they realized that their feelings for each other hadn't changed. They went to the marriage bureau in Naya's town. That night 150 of their friends gathered for an all-night party.

Upon graduation, Yeltsin had gone to work at the Urals Heavy Pipe Construction Trust. He and his wife now lived right next to the construction site. Soon their first child, a daughter named Lena, was born. Although he was overjoyed at the birth, Yeltsin had wanted a boy. Despite his preferences, a second daughter, Tanya, was born a couple of years later.

Yeltsin was 30 years old, with a growing family, when he joined the Communist Party in 1961. The party was the best avenue for career advancement in the old Soviet Union. He had spent one year after graduation obtaining experience in a wide variety of trades—as a carpenter, woodworker, glazier, plasterer, painter. By the end of the year, having mastered 12 specialized trades in the construction industry, he went to his boss and said that he was now ready to work as a foreman. Soon afterwards he found himself running a very large industrial complex that built five-story apartment houses. For the first time in his career, he was the man in charge. He seemed to relish the role.

Six feet tall, broad-shouldered, and with a shock of white hair, Yeltsin was an imposing presence radiating energy and forcefulness. He was known as a workaholic who managed to get by on four hours of sleep a night. In expressing his credo, Yeltsin once said: "Above all, I admire honesty, principle, and character. Correspondingly, I hate dishonesty and toadyism."

Hard work paid off for Yeltsin. In 1969, after 14 years in the construction industry, he received an invitation to head the section of the party's provincial committee responsible for construction. He was not surprised to receive the offer. He had been constantly engaged in party work outside working hours, and this was his reward.

In 1976, Yeltsin was sent by the party to Moscow to attend a two-week course at the Academy of Social Sciences. While there he was summoned to see then-Soviet leader Leonid Brezhnev. In the Kremlin, the ancient fortress that for three quarters of a century had been the heart of the world's largest Communist empire, Brezhnev was seated at the far end of a big conference table. He stood up as Yeltsin entered. Then he informed Yeltsin that he would be the next first party secretary of Sverdlovsk.

The province was a large one, with a correspondingly large party organization. Over the next several years Yeltsin gained a reputation as an energetic, charismatic reformer. It was during those years that he met Mikhail Gorbachev for the first time. They were both working as first secretaries, Gorbachev at Stavropol and Yeltsin at Sverdlovsk. Quite often they needed to lend each other a hand. In

> "Above all, I admire honesty, principle, and character. Correspondingly, I hate dishonesty and toadyism."

exchange for his Ural Mountain metals and timber, Yeltsin received much-needed food products from Gorbachev in Stavropol.

The two men were on fairly cordial terms, and in 1985, within five months of taking over as leader of the Soviet Union, Gorbachev invited Yeltsin to take the job of first party secretary of the Moscow City Party Committee. A party secretary's job was somewhat akin to that of an American mayor. Like big city mayors everywhere, Yeltsin wrestled with the problems of overpopulation, unemployment, housing shortages, crime, alcoholism, drug addiction, and inferior education. His real mandate from Gorbachev was to reform the corrupt city bureaucracy.

Yeltsin moved swiftly and gained notice among Muscovites. He encouraged the opening of street cafés and colorful fruit stalls to beautify a city that had grown gray and drab under other Communist leaders. Early in his tenure, he took to riding the city's buses and subways, talking to ordinary citizens about the problems of everyday life. Frequently he dropped in unannounced at city factories and stores, television cameras in tow, to note which goods were in short supply. When he found produce rotting in warehouses, he cut through red tape to ensure that vegetables would reach Moscow in fresh condition. For this alone, he gained great popular support.

By February 1986, Yeltsin was a nonvoting member of the Politburo, the Communist Party's inner decision-making body for the entire Soviet Union. He was gaining popular credibility and was now free to begin challenging the old guard Communists in the Politburo. That year, at the 27th Party Congress, he puzzled party insiders by taking himself to task for his own hypocrisy during the Brezhnev years. Yeltsin was practicing what he preached, issuing his own apologies, before taking aim at the higher Soviet leadership.

At Yeltsin's next big speech, to the Moscow City Party Committee, party functionaries were shocked to hear even more radical statements. He now talked openly about "pulling out the roots of bureaucracy, social injustice and abuses." Yeltsin argued against corrupt officials who reveled in special privileges, such as chauffeur-driven cars and special stores selling Western consumer goods unavailable to most Russians.

Yeltsin had clearly aligned himself with the reform wing of the Communist Party. What made him different from other politicians were his attacks on the self-satisfied bureaucrats who saw their jobs and privileges as virtual birthrights under communism. Not surprisingly, Yeltsin made enemies—as did Gorbachev, who was encountering resistance to *glasnost* and *perestroika.*

It didn't help that Yeltsin could be abrasive and hotheaded. Even his fellow reformers considered him gruff—but no one could have expected that he would take on Gorbachev. Yeltsin did so on October 26, 1987, on the 70th anniversary of the Russian Revolution that brought communism to power. At a plenum of the Central Committee, Gorbachev had just finished reading a draft of a speech he intended to deliver to the full Communist Party Central Committee. When Gorbachev was finished speaking, Yeltsin asked for the floor.

A flustered Gorbachev hesitated, then granted Yeltsin permission to speak. Yeltsin announced to the rather stunned audience that he had submitted letters of resignation on September 12 from both his Moscow Committee and his Politburo posts. Criticizing party leaders for inaction, he called Gorbachev's much-vaunted policy of *perestroika* a miserable failure. As far as the Russian people were concerned, he said, nothing good had come of these efforts. Yeltsin's daring speech was an extraordinary event in the

Soviet Union. A party insider had dared to openly criticize the leadership.

Yeltsin did not mention Gorbachev by name, though he did allude to a cult of personality that was threatening to derail economic restructuring. When he finished speaking, Yeltsin was viciously attacked. All 23 of his party comrades present at the plenum denounced Yeltsin for grandstanding and provoking what they said was an uncalled-for confrontation. Yeltsin rebutted, sticking to his charges against the Communist Party. Then Gorbachev spoke. The Soviet leader reprimanded Yeltsin for his "petty-bourgeois outburst" and labeled him a "political adventurist."

Muscovites first learned of the "Yeltsin affair" from foreign journalists. Not until three weeks later, on November 11, did Soviet television announce that the Moscow Party Committee had met that day and stripped Yeltsin of his post as first secretary. Two days later, the newspaper *Pravda* printed a three-page spread on the party meeting, stating that Yeltsin's personal ambitions had gotten the better of him. The article said that Gorbachev had called Yeltsin's speech "politically immature, extremely confusing, and contradictory."

Yeltsin, meanwhile, had been hospitalized with a heart ailment. On November 11 he was rushed to the Party Committee meeting, where he reportedly said, "I am guilty before the Moscow city party organization, Moscow City Party Committee, before you, and, of course, I am very guilty before Mikhail Sergeyevich Gorbachev."

Yeltsin's "confession" had a chilling effect on many supporters of Gorbachev's policy of *glasnost*, or openness, because hardly anyone believed that the proud Boris Yeltsin had actually made such a statement. The blatant campaign to discredit him revived images of forced apologies under the brutal dictator Joseph Stalin. Many analysts began to doubt the true openness of *glasnost*, noting that the full proceedings of the November 11 meeting had been released, but not Yeltsin's October 21 speech of accusation.

Unprecedented protest demonstrations erupted in Moscow. On November 17, several hundred students rallied at Moscow State University, demanding the publication of Yeltsin's October 21 speech to the Central Committee. Police broke up a meeting of the "Club of Social Initiatives," assembled in a Moscow factory to debate the Yeltsin affair. Demonstrations were also held in Leningrad and Sverdlovsk.

Yeltsin returned to the hospital immediately following the November 11th meeting. Early in 1988 he was dismissed from his Politburo post, but just days later he was offered the post of first deputy chairman of the State Committee for Construction. Yeltsin accepted. It was a demotion, but not a banishment to the provinces, and he was retained by the party's Central Committee.

The conciliatory gesture was not enough to keep Yeltsin quiet. His flair for public outbursts would continue. Soon he was quoted in the foreign press as calling the official version of his controversial "confession" an outright forgery. "I spoke out honestly and directly and said what I felt and thought was right," he later told the press. "I belong to those who are prepared to take the route with potholes, and have no fear of risks." In early May of 1988 he was quoted by a construction industry journal cautioning the party leadership on the importance of economic reform.

Finally, at the 19th All-Union Conference of the Communist Party of the Soviet Union, which was held in Moscow the last week of June 1988, he took to the floor and delivered a

> "I spoke out honestly and directly and said what I felt and thought was right. I belong to those who are prepared to take the route with potholes, and have no fear of risks."

stinging televised indictment of the party before five thousand delegates from all over the Soviet Union. Yeltsin ended his emotional speech by appealing for his own political rehabilitation: "Rehabilitation after 50 years has now become habitual," he said. "I am asking for political rehabilitation while I am still alive."

By now Gorbachev had heard quite enough from his junior comrade. In his closing remarks, he denounced Yeltsin for both his emotionalism and his political mistakes. Obviously, the request for rehabilitation had been denied. Yeltsin had "sullied" Gorbachev. In turn Gorbachev spurned Yeltsin, and it would prove to be a fateful decision. After the Soviet leadership approved changes in the country's constitution and a new legislature emerged, Boris Yeltsin would quickly become the first major leader to rise via the newly opened route of democracy and politics in the republics. The base of his popularity was Russia proper, the largest component of the Soviet Union.

The elections to the new Congress of People's Deputies, the 2,250-member upper house of Parliament, took place in the spring of 1989 amid evidence that many voters wanted to see reform move more quickly. Yeltsin was elected from Moscow with almost 90 percent of the vote.

It was the Soviet Union's first free election, and resulted in an overwhelming victory for Yeltsin and the forces of democracy. Soviet citizens had voted in multiparty elections for the first time. The results called for the Communist Party to surrender its monopoly on power in February 1990. In the course of 1990 practically all of the republics of the Soviet Union declared their "independence" from Moscow. The collapse of communism in other Eastern Europe countries had spread quickly during 1989. The new era had quickly spread beyond the Soviet borders.

In May 1990, Yeltsin was elected by his colleagues to lead the Russian parliament, becoming chairman of the Russian

Supreme Soviet—a position in the Russian Republic, not the Soviet Union. The legislature had elected Yeltsin chairman—or president—by a narrow four-vote margin on the third round of balloting. He now had a loftier platform for his tirades against the Kremlin's reluctance to introduce Western-style political and economic reform. He also demanded a popular vote on his presidency.

In the June 1991 elections, Yeltsin became the first president of the Russian Republic to be freely elected by the Russian people, winning more than half the vote. He had done what Gorbachev had refused to do—he had submitted himself directly to the people in a popular election. On July 10, he made his first speech as the new Russian president. "The great Russia is rising from its knees," he shouted to the cheering crowd. He assured them that they would have a democratic, peace-loving state, ruled by fair laws. "Russia will revive!" he vowed.

Yeltsin's remarkable rebirth in the Soviet Union's first free elections ensured both his worldwide fame and his position as the party elite's number-one enemy. The presidency of the Russian parliament, which was now separate from the Supreme Soviet of the Soviet Union, gave Yeltsin a powerful new platform from which to combat Gorbachev, who remained the president of the Soviet Union. It also touched off a "war of presidents," with the president of Russia and the president of the Soviet Union continually sniping at each other.

Despite Yeltsin's electoral landslide, there was a stubborn tendency in the West to dismiss him as a mere showoff who would not be around for long. Yet Yeltsin had fully recovered from mishaps that would have crushed the careers of most politicians. One of these mishaps was a

> "The great Russia is rising from its knees. Russia will revive!"

trip to the United States, where he was widely criticized, accused of drinking too much and acting like a boor. Another was a bizarre incident in which Yeltsin had turned up dripping wet at a Moscow police station with a semicoherent story about having been abducted and tossed in the Moscow River. The incident was never fully explained. The rumors involved drinking and a lover.

In dismissing Yeltsin, the West was overlooking a critical point. Throughout his evolution from Communist loyalist to radical reformer, Yeltsin had managed to keep the faith of the people. The majority of the Russian people, at least, seemed to believe that he was sincere in his efforts to fight for ordinary people. Back home, Yeltsin kept preaching accelerated reform, while Gorbachev was turning increasingly to a clutch of old-style party conservatives to run his government. Meanwhile, the economic state of the country was catastrophic. Living conditions were becoming intolerable.

Gorbachev and Yeltsin continued on a collision course throughout the spring and summer. In March of 1991 a pro-Yeltsin rally had been prevented when 50,000 troops sent by Gorbachev converged on Moscow. Five months later, on August 19, 1991, a group of hard-line conservatives in the Kremlin who wanted to halt reforms attempted a coup, putting Gorbachev under house arrest and declaring martial law. But the eight hard-line Communists were thwarted when Yeltsin, as president of Russia, went to Russia's own parliament building to demand popular resistance to the coup.

Parliament had remained in continuous session for three days as thousands of Russians gathered to defend their president and their parliament. Barricading himself inside the parliament building, Yeltsin called on the army to resist the coup. Visiting him at the parliament building, known as the Russian White House, the Russian Orthodox Patriarch

On August 19, 1991, Boris Yeltsin makes a speech from atop a tank in front of the Russian parliament building in Moscow. (AP/Wide World Photos)

of Moscow sided with Yeltsin. Soon a good number of ordinary Russians made their communions there and vowed to shed their blood for freedom.

Overall, however, the situation was still quite desperate. Only a small contingent of elite troops had sided with Yeltsin. The Russian White House could be taken fairly easily. Tanks rolling into Moscow were still undecided about which side they were on, and Yeltsin was expecting an attack of overwhelming force at any moment.

While holed up in the White House, Yeltsin glanced out the window. He noticed an armored vehicle surrounded by a crowd. He saw that people were not afraid to approach the tanks. They were even lining up. They weren't afraid of being arrested, although they were being threatened with a crackdown every hour over the radio and television. Suddenly Yeltsin felt a jolt of emotion. He had to go out there right away. He had to be standing with the people. By doing so, he would be standing up to the coup plotters who were holding Gorbachev captive in the Crimea. Yeltsin's instincts were right. When he emerged courageously from the parliament building to greet throngs of jubilant supporters, he seized the golden moment of his political life—and created one of the most remarkable moments in all of Russian history.

Yeltsin clambered aboard one of the tanks and stood up tall. He talked to the soldiers outside the parliament building. He even greeted the astonished commander of the tank he was standing on. "From their faces, from the expression in their eyes, I could see they would not shoot us," he later recalled. Yeltsin jumped off the tank and was back inside the White House in minutes. He knew the tide had turned in his favor. He knew that when he stood atop the tank, in one grand gesture of defiance, the coup was doomed.

It was indeed. The Soviet high command sensed the mood of the people and sided with Yeltsin. At that point, the rest of the army command saw that they could not prevail without massive bloodshed. In the face of popular resistance led by Yeltsin, the coup had quickly disintegrated. Thus ended three of the most unforgettable days in Soviet history. The image of Yeltsin, unarmed, in his civilian suit, standing on a tank, will always symbolize what became known as the second Russian revolution.

> "From their faces, from the expression in their eyes, I could see they would not shoot us."

The defeat of the coup was a global event, and Yeltsin was the man of the hour. Euphoric throngs danced in the streets outside the Russian parliament building. Gorbachev, who had returned from 72 hours in captivity in his lavish dacha (country house), looked haggard and tired when he appeared the next day before the Russian parliament. The Soviet president thanked the Russian president for his heroic stand. Gorbachev was speaking when Yeltsin stepped to the podium. He wagged a finger of disapproval at Gorbachev, scolding him for having trusted his government to a clutch of Communist hard-liners. Yeltsin insisted that Gorbachev read aloud the names of the coup plotters who, days before, had been his closest friends.

After the shock of the coup, all the Union republics voted to secede from the Soviet Union. The Soviet Union ceased to exist as a nation—one of the most influential and important events of the century. Yeltsin became the president of an independent Russia. He had to contend with an economy that was in total collapse—a rubble that was Russia's inheritance from nearly 75 years of communism. He didn't have the luxury of carrying out democratic political reform and liberal economic reform separately. He had to gamble and attempt to do it all at once.

Immediately after the August 1991 coup, Yeltsin banned the presence of the Communist Party in the workplace and confiscated its property. Some democrats urged that the Russian Congress of People's Deputies and its standing parliament, the Supreme Soviet, also be abolished and new elections held. Yeltsin decided against this, a choice later considered to be one of his great mistakes. Indeed it proved to be, for the old parliament was left in place, and Russian democracy began without a legal constitution.

Yeltsin also had to contend with the country's loss of world power and prestige—a loss that was unsettling to most Russians in the wake of the collapse of the Soviet Union. The sentiment was only aggravated by Russia's new dependence on the West. Yeltsin immediately moved to reorient Russia's foreign policy away from the Soviet quest for global power. He pragmatically negotiated with the West such delicate issues as nuclear arms cuts. Still Yeltsin was plagued in his first year as president by the abysmal state of the economy, which was in the deepest decline in a slide that had begun under Brezhnev and accelerated under Gorbachev.

During 1991 the parliament became the vehicle for conservative opposition to all of Yeltsin's reforms. He decided that only a clean break with the old order could save the economy. He announced his commitment to this radical course of action on October 18, 1991. Yeltsin's initial aim was not to jump-start the economy, but to destroy the old command-administrative system. He set out to create an "irreversible situation" that would make it impossible to return to the old order.

The economic program he put in place in January 1992 was not in fact the full "shock therapy" that had been prescribed to revive the ailing economy. Artificial price controls, a fixture of the Soviet economy, were lifted, though not on food staples, transportation, or energy. Industrial managers led the opposition to real prices, demanding a return to subsidies from the government to prop up industries. Everywhere, it seemed, the pain of economic decline led to pleas that Yeltsin adopt a more "gradual" course.

The problem was that former party apparatchiks still managed the large state enterprises that made up the economy. As a result, the government lost control of the money supply, and economic stability was threatened. It would have been political suicide for Yeltsin to let state enterprises fail and unemployment grow too quickly, before new opportunities were created. Yeltsin was learning how difficult it was to govern.

Reform continued, though at a slow pace, right through the December elections to the parliament. The national campaign, the first in Russia's history, at times seemed like a circus. While pop stars, athletes, and grandmothers joined conventional politicians on the ballot, dangerous demagogues attacked the status quo. Yeltsin, however, did not participate in the campaign. His uncharacteristic silence is something he most likely later regretted.

At the height of the 1993 campaign, Yeltsin decided to dissolve the parliament by presidential decree, arguing that it was controlled by old-guard Communists who had never been freely elected. Yeltsin's action led to a crisis in which Russia's newborn democracy was once again compromised. When the rebellious parliament defied Yeltsin's order to dissolve, he ordered his tanks to form a ring around the parliament building.

The blockade, which began on September 24, reached a climax on Sunday, October 3. The next morning Yeltsin learned that rebel factions of the armed forces had broken the blockade and seized the parliament building. Now they were threatening to descend on Moscow in large detachments. Hundreds of people had been issued guns. Russia was again drowning in lawlessness.

Like the coup attempt two years before, the rebellion might have succeeded were it not for Yeltsin's personal intervention. When he drove to the Defense Ministry that morning, the army appeared unable or unwilling to do anything. One army general told Yeltsin that he was reluctant to take the building by force. Another general said there was a shortage of troops. Not satisfied, Yeltsin resorted to having a junior officer execute a plan.

The Kremlin's security chief, Captain Mikhail Barsukov, had been deeply involved in the defense of the parliament building in August 1991. When he reviewed the options for assaulting the building through underground tunnels, Yeltsin's generals suddenly came alive. Tanks were called out. The parliamentary uprising against Yeltsin was no better planned or conducted than the coup two years before. The building was stormed and captured. The mutiny was crushed. And civil war was averted.

The elections went ahead as scheduled. The results on December 12, 1993, were a shock to both Yeltsin and the world. Yeltsin's reformers won only 35 percent of the seats.

Yeltsin's opponents carried 45 percent of the vote. The election results meant that a powerful bloc of Vladimir Zhirinovsky's party (a so-called democratic party that wanted to impose military dictatorship) and the new Communists could stop Yeltsin's reform efforts. Yeltsin's major victory was passage of the constitution, the one thing he had campaigned for, but the response of the electorate was bewildering.

Yeltsin emerged from isolation to say that the people had voted not against him, but against the bad economic conditions. He retracted a pledge to hold early presidential elections, and then made a shocking statement. He said that after he served out the remainder of his term—due to expire in 1996—he would not run again. "Everyone knows how many blows I've taken," Yeltsin said. "For one person, it's too much."

All was not well with Yeltsin and his new democracy. At the close of 1995, the country was paralyzed by a hostage crisis in the southern breakaway region of Cechnya. Yeltsin's approval rating had plummeted to the 4-to-8 percent range, and he was busy firing the free-market reformers in his cabinet. So when he roused himself and decided to run, his astonishing come-from-behind victory in the June 1996 elections was the story of an aging leader who was nevertheless Russia's only hope against a return of communism. That fact was evident throughout his campaign when Yeltsin was again hospitalized with heart problems. His hospital stay fueled speculation about his health and his viability as a presidential candidate. His energy seemed to be fading and he was increasingly detached from the political process, though he has restored his reformist agenda.

Whatever his future, Yeltsin's legacy is massive. The first democratically elected—and re-elected (by 54 percent of the vote)—president in the history of Russia unleashed the entrepreneurial spirit among the population, especially the young people. Russia finally changed, and almost entirely because of the bold steps he dared to take. Never had change in Russia been more rapid than in Yeltsin's first year. In his wake, and for the foreseeable future, the process of democratization can no longer be stopped, only slowed.

"A man must live like a great bright flame and burn as brightly as he can," Yeltsin once said. "In the end, he burns out. But this is better than a little flame." Yet, says Yeltsin biographer Craig Miller, democracy "must outlast the span of a single human life if a country is to prosper under it. Future generations will not determine Boris Yeltsin's place in history by the brightness of his own flame. All that will matter is whether the fire he lit for democracy in Russia will continue to burn."

Chronology

February 1, 1931	Born in Butko, Sverdlovsk Province, Russian Republic, U.S.S.R.
1955	Graduates from Urals Polytechnic Institute, where he studied civil engineering
1956	Marries Naya Girina
1961	Joins the Communist Party
1969	Becomes a full-time Communist Party official, responsible for all construction in Sverdlovsk
1976	Becomes first secretary of Sverdlovsk Province, a step up the ladder in the Communist Party
December 24, 1985	Becomes first party secretary of the Moscow City Party committee of the Communist Party
February 18, 1986	Chosen a nonvoting member of the Politburo, the real center of power in the Communist Party

September 12, 1987	Writes letter of resignation, asking to be removed from his position in the Politburo and the Moscow City Committee
October 21, 1987	At a plenum of the Central Committee, asks to be relieved of his duties. Criticizes party leaders for inaction. His speech is followed by verbal attacks against him from other committee members in what would become known as the Yeltsin Affair
November 11, 1987	Called from his hospital bed to attend a meeting of the Moscow City Committee, where he is attacked politically by other party members. In the end he is stripped of his post as first secretary. Surprisingly, just days later, Gorbachev offers him post of first deputy chairman of the State Committee for Construction. Yeltsin accepts
June 1988	Public rallies to Yeltsin's defense after attack against him at the 19th Party Conference
March 26, 1989	In the first free elections since 1917, Yeltsin is voted into the Congress of People's Deputies, winning 89.6 percent of the vote
May 25, 1989	Mikhail Gorbachev becomes president of the U.S.S.R.
May 1990	Yeltsin elected to lead the Russian parliament, becoming chairman of the Russian Supreme Soviet (a position in the Russian Republic, not the U.S.S.R.)
June 12, 1991	Becomes the first president of the Russian Republic to be elected directly by the people, winning more than half the vote
August 1991	Becomes a hero when, with the support of the Russian people, he overthrows a coup attempt by hard-line Communists

December 22, 1991	The Soviet Union unravels when 11 former republics agree to join Yeltsin's new commonwealth. Three days later, Gorbachev resigns as president of the U.S.S.R.
January 2, 1992	Yeltsin removes government controls on prices of goods. Prices soar
October 1993	Orders troops to storm parliament building, crushing second hard-line coup attempt in as many years
December 12, 1993	Elections shock Yeltsin when opponents win a large block of votes
July 1995	Hospitalized for heart problems
June 16, 1996	Wins by 54 percent of the vote to become the first democratically elected Russian president to be re-elected

Further Reading

Ayer, Eleanor. *Boris Yeltsin: A Man of the People.* New York: Dillon Press, 1992. Traces the life of the Russian leader from his childhood on a collective farm through his education as a civil engineer to his election as the first president of the Russian Republic in 1991.

Kallen, Stuart A. *Gorbachev-Yeltsin: The Fall of Communism.* Edina, Minn.: Abdo and Daughters, 1992. Examines the events in the Soviet Union during the time of Yeltsin and Gorbachev, including the failed coup of 1991 and the collapse of the Soviet Union itself.

Schecter, Kate. *Boris Yeltsin.* New York: Chelsea House, 1994. Traces the life of the Russian leader from his impoverished childhood, through his political career, to his role in the 1991 coup, and the beginning of his presidency.

Mikhail Gorbachev, former president of the Soviet Union. (UPP/Photoreporters, Inc.)

Mikhail Gorbachev

On coming to power in the Soviet Union in 1985, Communist Party chief Mikhail Gorbachev launched a series of earthshaking changes that nobody could have foreseen. The people of his country were given back the right to think and speak freely, as taboos were lifted that had held the population—occupants of one-sixth of the world's land mass—in fear for most of the 20th century. The new freedom brought miracles abroad and helped lead to the collapse of communism at home and in the Soviet Union's Eastern European satellite states.

Seven years after coming to power, Gorbachev tried to steer a middle course between the Soviet Union's reformist democrats and recalcitrant Communists—and wound up despised by both camps. For three days a group of bungling hard-line Communists placed Gorbachev under house arrest at his dacha—his country home—in the Crimea, but the coup plotters failed to overthrow his government. When he returned to Moscow three days later, Gorbachev was yesterday's man. Russia had a new man of the hour, Gorbachev's chief rival, Boris Yeltsin. Within months the Soviet Union collapsed and Gorbachev was forced to resign the presidency of a country that no longer existed.

Mikhail Sergeyevich Gorbachev was born March 2, 1931, in a small clay-and-wood house in the peasant village of Privolnoye. His home was nestled in a fertile farm region of southern Russia, just north of the Caucasus Mountains, in the southwest corner of the Soviet Union. Life was never exactly easy for Misha, as he was known, but it was better than for most peasant boys at the time. His father drove a combine harvester on a state farm, a job that carried a much higher status than an ordinary farm hand.

At birth, Misha had solid credentials for a rise through the ranks of the Communist Party. His grandfather Andrei was the chairman of the local collective farm and a trusted party loyalist. As a result, his family survived the famines, executions, and imprisonments that were the fate of many other peasants who resisted Stalin. A purge of local party organizations did touch his extended family when his maternal grandfather was arrested—but Misha's grandfather was one of the lucky ones. He was freed after spending only a year and a half in jail.

Misha was only 11 when the Germans occupied the Stavropol region during World War II. Though the fighting had not reached Stavropol until 1945, a local war memorial contains the names of seven Gorbachevs who lost their lives to the Nazis. The fighting never reached Misha's small village of Privolnoye, but it came close enough that his parents pulled him out of school for three months.

Misha returned to school, though under severe conditions. He had to hike 10 miles a day, often through freezing snow. Even the determined and ambitious Misha found this hard to bear. To ease the hardships, his father rented him an unheated room near school for 150 rubles a year. It was a large sum for an ordinary Soviet citizen, but Misha was worth the sacrifice. He had worked hard at his studies. He was an eager student who always answered the toughest of questions. According to his high school principal, he "also gave the most elaborate answers."

Misha was a student who always found time for extracurricular activities. As a member of the drama club, he even played the czar in one show. On graduation, he was awarded a silver medal, his school's second highest academic honor. By this stage in his life he had already begun to secure his future in Soviet society. A high school essay he wrote was entitled "Stalin Is the Glory of our Country, Stalin Is the Youth." The politically correct essay received the top grade.

The essay was the beginning of Gorbachev's long political march to Moscow. When he joined the Young Communist League—the Komsomol—at the age of 14, Misha donated his time generously and established himself as an articulate and enthusiastic supporter of party goals. As a young man who almost always made the most of the opportunities that came his way, Misha would eventually become the leader of the Komsomol.

To help support his family, Misha had to work especially hard in the grain-covered hills surrounding his tiny village. The summer of 1946 was the first of four he would spend working at a machine and tractor station as an assistant driver of a combine harvester. The job at the collective farm became full-time for one year after high school. It was the way his father had always made a living. Now father and son worked side by side all day long, both spattered with mud in the scorching-hot grain fields. In the winter months, when Misha drove the combine, he had to drape himself with straw to keep out the cold and freezing wind. The harvest in 1949 was a stellar one, and Gorbachev shared in the success of his hard work.

Gorbachev began to set his sights on Moscow. Instead of taking the safe route, and going to a university in his province, he applied and was accepted to Moscow State University, the country's leading institution of higher learning.

Gorbachev knew that staying in Stavropol might limit his future in a country where all power was centralized in faraway Moscow. So he moved to Moscow, the largest city in the country, a thousand miles away. On the train he saw with his own eyes the terrible suffering his country had endured during World War II. The war had been over for five years, but much of the countryside was still in ruins.

At Moscow State University, which he entered in 1950, Gorbachev invested more energy in politics than in his studies. He was an average student who did well in a number of subjects, but he was not brilliant in any of them. He quickly settled on the study of law, which seemed an odd choice, since very few students studied the law. It was not a particularly prestigious calling in the Soviet Union at the time. Primarily, studying the law was considered good preparation for a career in the party.

Gorbachev was a typical new student, living in a crowded complex that held more than 190,000 students. The gigantic dormitory in the middle of Moscow, once a military barracks built by Czar Peter the Great, held 6 to 16 students crammed into each room. The dorm was coed, although men and women lived in separate rooms.

At the university Gorbachev met people from all over the Soviet Union and Europe. It was the first time he had gotten to know people from outside his small farming village. He got along well with his roommates, one of whom was a Czech named Zdenek Mlynar. Gorbachev talked endlessly with his Czech friend, and learned about Western-style life. Gorbachev staunchly defended communism as superior to capitalism. But once, when the two students had gone to see a Soviet propaganda movie that painted a flattering picture of life on a collective, Gorbachev told Mlynar that he thought the movie was wrong.

While maintaining faith in the communism he was weaned on, Gorbachev was showing the first signs of what later would be a full-blown zeal to correct the corrupt and inefficient Soviet system. He was convinced that reform could be done from within, by working through the Communist Party system. He would always remain a child of the Soviet 1960s, a generation that still believed Marxism-Leninism could be melded with the democracy and market forces of the West.

Moving up through the Komsomol, the traditional training group for Soviet party officials, he became a Komsorg, or Komsomol leader, of his class at the university. Within two years Gorbachev was Komsomol leader of the whole law school. He was quite popular because of his clowning abilities. It was impossible, however, for Gorbachev, in his one ill-fitting suit, to hide his country bumpkin origins among the sophisticated student body in Moscow.

One night he went to a dancing school intending to poke fun at some of his friends who were taking lessons. There he met a striking, elegant woman name Raisa Titornko. Raisa was a philosophy student who possessed a quick and challenging intellect. The couple enjoyed reading and studying together. They were married during Gorbachev's last year at the university. The couple celebrated with singing and dancing in Gorbachev's dorm room. For the next few months, the two newlyweds lived separately until they could find a room in a residential hall for married students.

On graduation, Gorbachev returned to Stavropol with his law degree and immersed himself in party work. He worked from 1956 to 1958 as first secretary of the Stavropol city Komsomol organization. After that he served the Komsomol committee for the Stavropol territory, first as deputy chief of the propaganda department, then as second secretary, and later as first secretary. By 1963 he had worked his way up to chief of the agricultural department for the entire Stavropol region.

It was an important post for someone so young. Gorbachev was rising steadily in the Communist hierarchy throughout the 1960s, obtaining a degree in agronomy before being chosen as first party secretary of his whole region. At 39, he had become one of the youngest provincial party chiefs in the entire U.S.S.R. Gorbachev eagerly threw himself into the job, taking initiatives that pleased the peasants. He expanded the size of private plots and gave the collectives a greater voice in planning. Soon his innovations attracted the attention of party authorities in Moscow.

Gorbachev was rewarded with a new post as a deputy to the Soviet of the Union within the bicameral Supreme Soviet—the formal legislative body of the U.S.S.R. Everyone could see that he was a fast-rising star in national politics. Within the national party organization, he became a member of the powerful Central Committee in 1971. As a Central Committee member, he served as a delegate to a number of party congresses in the U.S.S.R. and was sent on several trips abroad.

Even the most promising Soviet party officials needed friends to help propel their careers. Gorbachev was no exception. He found favor with Mikhail A. Suslov, a former Stavropol party chief who served as Leonid Brezhnev's ideology minister, and with KGB chairman Yuri Andropov, a member of the Suslov faction in the Kremlin. With their blessings, Gorbachev joined the Kremlin's inner circle in November 1978 as agricultural secretary of the 10-member Secretariat of the party's Central Committee.

While the appointment gave him a big leg up in the Soviet succession ladder, it was a hazardous assignment—the sad state of Soviet agriculture was the Achilles' heel of the Soviet economy. Many party leaders had already failed to boost production. In a position traditionally fraught with career risks, Gorbachev would push forward.

To decentralize planning, he transferred control over agricultural production from the ministries in Moscow to the regional authorities. Gorbachev also adopted a "brigade system" that assigned workers to specific plots of land and rewarded them with increased pay if they could boost their production. But his reforms had little effect. A shrinking amount of arable land and an uncertain climate made for poor harvests. Despite his innovations, Gorbachev fared no better than his predecessors.

The failing harvests did not, however, damage his career. Party loyalty meant more than accomplishments in the Soviet system. Besides, many leaders, among them Nikita Khrushchev, had failed as agriculture secretaries. So Gorbachev, the "Teflon commissar," as *Newsweek* called him, continued to advance his career under the patronage of Suslov and Andropov. The next year, when he was advanced to a full voting Politburo membership, change was in the wind. Within three years, Gorbachev would reach the peak of his power.

Gorbachev's meteoric rise began when Brezhnev died in 1982. Gorbachev's long-time mentor, Yuri Andropov, was elected to replace him as general secretary. Of course, Gorbachev was excited about playing an active role in advancing Andropov's reformist wishes. He helped Andropov purge the government of thousands of corrupt and incompetent party bureaucrats. He also supervised Andropov's high-profile "five ministries" program, an effort to give industrial managers greater flexibility in establishing production goals.

Both inside and outside the walls of the Kremlin, Gorbachev was increasingly seen as one of Andropov's closest aides. As Andropov's health began to fail, Gorbachev became the ailing leader's liaison with the outside world. Gorbachev was now making major speeches for Andropov and attending important diplomatic functions. Obviously, he was being groomed by Andropov for succession as general secretary. But when Andropov died, the hidebound old guard passed over Gorbachev. Apparently he was still considered too young and inexperienced for the job of Communist Party chief. Instead of Gorbachev, the elderly and ailing Konstantin Chernenko, an old Brezhnev loyalist, was named the next Soviet leader.

Gorbachev, however, emerged from the succession struggle in a very strong position. He supported Chernenko loyally. He was wise not to push him out. He just waited for him either to die or fade away. Gradually Gorbachev began to take charge of more and more of Chernenko's public leadership functions. On the world stage he displayed a sense of humor and a grace that were refreshing changes from the deadly somber tone of old Soviet leaders.

It was no surprise that Gorbachev was the clear choice to succeed Chernenko. Only a few hours after the announcement of Chernenko's death, on March 11, 1985, Gorbachev was elected general secretary in an emergency meeting of the Central Committee. The speed of his confirmation suggested to the outside world that his appointment as the next leader of the Soviet Union had been arranged for some time. At 54, having risen through the Communist system of the Soviet Union, he had become the absolute ruler of the only nation competing with the United States for world supremacy.

The accession of Gorbachev was greeted with enormous hope at home and abroad. With the consecutive deaths of Brezhnev, Andropov, and Chernenko, the old guard had expired. "Gorby," as he became known, represented an infusion of new blood into the crusty Soviet leadership. In making his acceptance speech on the same day as Chernenko's death, Gorbachev emphasized rapid economic development as the most important goal and called for "further perfection and development of democracy" and "socialist self-government."

His rise to the post of general secretary of the Communist Party was taken as a major turning point in the history of the Soviet Union—and of the world. The youngest Soviet leader since Joseph Stalin succeeded Lenin in 1924, Gorbachev seemed articulate, well-educated, and confident.

To Russians, his youth and vitality represented a dramatic change. And the new gospel he preached—of *glasnost* or openness—was unlike anything heard since the 1970s period of detente between East and West. Moreover, his talk was backed up by action and change. Gorbachev invited the great dissident and scientist Andrei D. Sakharov to return to Moscow from exile. Hundreds of other dissidents, like Anatoly Scharansky, were allowed to emigrate. The arts bloomed and religious faiths were freely practiced. Intellectuals sang the praises of the new leader. Dissidents in China and Eastern Europe made Gorbachev's name a rallying cry.

Beginning in 1988, legislation initiated by Gorbachev under his plan for *perestroika*, an economic restructuring plan, transferred a major part of economic responsibility from the government to individual enterprises. The change removed much of the financial security that Soviet workers were used to, and as Gorbachev's novelty wore off, his popularity at home began to slip. Russians impatient with the pace of *perestroika* resented him for essentially staying the course of reform begun by his mentor Andropov. He seemed satisfied with economic and social tinkering rather than a complete overhaul. As a dyed-in-the-wool Communist, he did not want to dismantle the system of centralized planning.

Enforcing greater worker discipline and rewarding effort with cash bonuses and consumer goods was Gorbachev's idea of economic revitalization. But as it had in recent years, the Soviet economy continued to sputter, even showing alarming signs of weakness here and there. By his first anniversary in office Gorbachev was already attempting to eliminate unnecessary bureaucrats and red tape. As general secretary of the Communist Party, he did what he could to clean house. He forced the retirement of many officials, mostly protégés of his predecessors.

On the world stage, meanwhile, he leaned toward a peaceful but tough course of coexistence with the United States. The combination of a friendly manner and a tenaciousness in pursuing goals served him well. What was said of Gorbachev at his acceptance speech was often repeated abroad. "He has a nice smile, but he has teeth of iron." But many analysts believed that Gorbachev's domestic problems were too pressing for him to take any assertive action in foreign affairs. That might have threatened the uneasy state of relations with the West.

Nevertheless, he demonstrated a knack for diplomatic showmanship. On Easter Sunday in 1985 he announced that the Soviet Union would observe a six-month moratorium on deployment of its SS-20 medium-range nuclear missiles. He also came out strongly against the proposed Strategic Defense Initiative, or "Star Wars" plan, of the United States, which he regarded as a dangerous militarization of space. Although Gorbachev denounced the United States as "the forward edge of the war menace to mankind," he called the superpower rivalry "an anomaly." At the Moscow trade talks in May 1985 he told U.S. Secretary of Commerce Malcolm Baldridge that it was "high time to defrost the potential for Soviet-American cooperation."

Eight months after coming to power, in November 1985, Gorbachev met in Geneva with U.S. President Ronald Reagan. Under Gorbachev's "new thinking," Soviet foreign policy had done a sharp turnaround. Gorbachev greatly reduced nuclear arsenals. He brought the Soviet Union's war with Afghanistan to an end. With his blessing, East and West Germany were reunited, and the Iron Curtain that divided East from West came down.

After five years as president, Gorbachev had accomplished many of his goals, but many Russians felt that he was not moving quickly enough on economic reform. His chief rival, Boris Yeltsin, began to accuse him of being too slow with his reforms. Instead of heeding Yeltsin, Gorbachev dismissed him in November 1987. It was a fateful decision. Cut off from all traditional sources of power, spurning the party, Yeltsin would become Gorbachev's chief political foe.

Gorbachev's goal of *perestroika* had proved extremely difficult to achieve. Gorbachev, meanwhile, became the prime exponent of using the media to give object lessons in the new politics. In a nationally televised session of the 19th Party Conference in June 1988, he bluntly told the nation: "*Perestroika* is not manna from heaven. Instead of waiting for it to be brought in from somewhere, it must be brought about by the people—themselves."

Virtually all the economic statistics were grim. Because of a failed system of distribution that Gorbachev inherited from his predecessors, nearly one third of all produce rotted before it reached consumers. Changes backed by Gorbachev did not call for the breakup of the collective farm system, but under the new system farmers would be able to lease land and equipment from collectives and grow what they chose. Nor would they be required to sell all their produce on the state market.

Few leaders, and certainly no Soviet leaders, had attained the level of international popularity Gorbachev had by the beginning of 1989. His visit to New York and his speech to the United Nations in December 1988 had gone well. In February of 1989, the Soviet military withdrawal from Afghanistan was completed,

> "*Perestroika* is not manna from heaven. Instead of waiting for it to be brought in from somewhere, it must be brought about by the people—themselves."

clearing away a major impediment to better relations between the Soviet Union and the rest of the world.

In domestic politics, on the surface at least, Gorbachev appeared to be consolidating his power. At his behest, the Supreme Soviet in December 1988 had approved changes in the constitution that provided for a new legislature. The 2,250-member upper house, the Congress of People's Deputies, would be chosen through elections in which candidates could run against each other. This was a dramatic departure from the era of hand-picked party stalwarts who ran unopposed.

As the election approached, Gorbachev traveled the country, campaigning for his programs. In a nationally televised encounter with ordinary citizens on the streets of Kiev, he urged the country to continue on the path of reform: "Press on comrades—we from above, you from below. This is the only way *perestroika* can happen. Just like a vise. If there's pressure from only one side, it won't work."

When Soviet citizens voted for the first time in multiparty elections in 1989, the results of a referendum called for the Communist Party to surrender its monopoly on power in February 1990. The contests for election to the Congress also saw the defeat of a number of veteran Communist Party stalwarts, amid evidence that many voters wished to see Gorbachev implement reforms more quickly. Boris Yeltsin, who for years had been scolding Gorbachev for moving too slowly with economic reform, was elected to the Congress from Moscow with 90 percent of the vote.

By his fifth anniversary in power, Gorbachev was on the defensive for clinging to his Communist ideologies.

> "Press on comrades—we from above, you from below. This is the only way *perestroika* can happen. Just like a vise. If there's pressure from only one side, it won't work."

His conduct of domestic affairs seemed hesitant and half-hearted. People now grumbled more openly about the failed promises of economic reform. His supporters argued even more loudly that Gorbachev required a popular mandate through national presidential elections to gather the strength necessary for the radical reforms needed to save the economy. Instead, Gorbachev sought and acquired a more powerful executive presidency for himself, without ever submitting his name to the voters in a popular election.

During October and November of 1990 the tide of affairs began to run against him. Gorbachev's popularity had fallen to 20 percent in the opinion polls. He got no boost from the Nobel Peace Prize he received on October 15. The day after winning the award, Gorbachev withdrew his support for the 500 Days economic reform plan, a program designed to revive the Soviet economy through harsh sacrifices that would result in a lower standard of living for most Russians.

Gorbachev's withdrawal of support made it clear to everyone in the Soviet Union that he had begun swinging to the conservative side. Radical economic reformers who wanted to speed the transition to a market economy were shocked at Gorbachev's action. They accused him of caving in to the military hard-liners who had everything to lose from the reform of the country. Soon Gorbachev would reject all the reformers on his team. It was probably his worst, most dangerous mistake, because what followed was nothing short of war.

Gorbachev was at odds with the popular Soviet politician Boris Yeltsin. In March of 1991, when a pro-Yeltsin rally was scheduled, 50,000 troops sent by Gorbachev converged on Moscow to prevent any activity. In May Gorbachev was humiliated by jeering crowds during the May Day celebration in Red Square. Yeltsin, who had been fired by Gorbachev in 1988 as chief of Moscow's Communist Party, was gaining widespread popularity as the standard-bearer for radicals anxious for faster changes in the Soviet parliament. On June 12, Yeltsin emerged triumphant as president of the vast Russian Republic. With that election, Gorbachev lost to Yeltsin his leadership of more than half of the Soviet Union's 280 million people.

The election also gave Yeltsin, as president of the Russian Republic, a formidable power base from which to challenge the Soviet president, Gorbachev. This set off a "war of presidents" between the two men.

For a brief moment in time Gorbachev seemed to have regained his footing, if not his popularity. At a Central Committee meeting in July 1991, Gorbachev was encouraged that conservatives formerly opposed to change now voted for all his measures—including a mixed economy, private property, religious freedom, and freedom for writers and thinkers from "ideological and administrative dictatorship." Then, quite suddenly, during the second half of August, a clutch of these same conservatives tried to seize power. On August 19, the very conservatives Gorbachev had brought into the Kremlin showed their true colors. They turned on Gorbachev while he was on vacation in the Crimea, placing him under house arrest and declaring martial law.

The coup was a pathetic undertaking, badly planned by eight bungling hard-liners who were oblivious to the degree to which fear had been lifted from society during the six years of *glasnost*. It quickly disintegrated in the face of popular resistance led by Yeltsin, who defended the Russian parliament. When Gorbachev returned to Moscow from 72 hours in captivity, it seemed a golden moment for him. But once again, the fast pace of events seemed to elude him. Instead of rushing to greet the euphoric throngs outside the Russian parliament and embracing Yeltsin and the new era that had opened up, Gorbachev did not appear until a news conference the next day.

With the party in disgrace and the Union in disarray, his return to Moscow from the Crimea was not a triumph. Gorbachev's chief problem was that he failed to see that people had stood up not for him, but for the freedoms he had enabled them to take. When he appeared before the public for the first time he talked of the coup as an attack against him personally. "The President of the country was isolated from the country and the world. The objective was to crush the President morally, to crush his family, but they failed," he said.

Gorbachev did appear on television to thank the Russian people and Boris Yeltsin, but evidently he didn't realize that public opinion had completely changed. He promised to purge the Communist Party, but said he was still a Communist, a statement that was met with disbelief among Russians. While he was speaking, Yeltsin stepped to the podium and publicly scolded Gorbachev. During the televised exchange, the tired-looking president was forced by Yeltsin to read a list of coup backers—a "who's who" of the Soviet establishment.

It was the most humiliating moment of Gorbachev's career. Yeltsin pointed his finger and demanded that Gorbachev obey him. In that instant, Gorbachev's image was permanently altered and his fate was sealed. A week before, he had been a reformer of the old order. Now he was seen as an obstacle in the way of a new order, led by a new leader.

Gorbachev was forced to carry out a much more drastic purge of the Communist Party than he had in-

> "The President of the country was isolated from the country and the world. The objective was to crush the President morally, to crush his family, but they failed."

tended. He was compelled by Yeltsin to cancel appointments he had made to the Ministry of Defense. Trusted Yeltsin reformers were put in their place. At subsequent meetings, Gorbachev showed a new face. He broke with the Communist Party completely. Unleashing in quick succession a series of measures that seemed to conjure up the Gorbachev of the summer past, he suspended the party, dismissed his cabinet, purged the KGB, and recognized the three Baltic republics of the former Soviet Union as separate nations. It was a case of too little, too late.

On August 24, 1991, Gorbachev resigned as general secretary of the party. He remained president, though not by popular election. In this post-coup period, he even had a last hurrah on the international stage when he matched President George Bush's sweeping cuts in tactical nuclear weapons in early October. On December 25, 1991, Gorbachev bowed to the inevitable. He finally resigned as president after almost seven years of reforms.

His leadership actually ended four days before that, in the Kazakh capital of Alma Ata in Central Asia, when the leaders of the 11 former Soviet republics formally signed a declaration founding the Commonwealth of Independent States. In doing so, they declared that the Soviet Union no longer existed. Gorbachev's job as president was abolished.

> "The old system fell apart even before the new system began to work."

In a 10-minute television broadcast, Gorbachev said that he had no regrets whatsoever about the democratic reform movement he had launched, but added: "The old system fell apart even before the new system began to work." He said he supported the independence of the republics but opposed "dismembering this country and disuniting the states," a reference to the Commonwealth of Independent States that had been formed the week before.

As Gorbachev spoke, the red flag was lowered from the Kremlin. But the change was more than symbolic. Control of the Soviet nuclear arsenal passed to Yeltsin of Russia. Finally, the Russian people voted to replace Gorbachev with Yeltsin. Ironically, it was one of the first triumphs of the fragile democracy that Gorbachev had done so much to nurture.

Today Gorbachev is a private citizen, traveling frequently and speaking around the world. He has made no secret of his desire to return to political office. So far, however, there has not been even the faintest call from the Russian people. Almost five years after finding himself out of a job, Gorbachev remains one of the most disliked politicians in Russia.

His defeat as a candidate in the June 1996 elections was resounding. Gorbachev had become a fringe political figure with the slimmest chance of redeeming himself in the eyes of the Russians he helped set free.

Yet the fact remains that no one influenced the politics of today's world more than Mikhail Gorbachev. At the same time, events forced Gorbachev to change profoundly. He injected the first notes of freedom into a society where secrecy, repression, and disinformation were pervasive—by promoting *glasnost* and *perestroika*, releasing dissidents, and giving accurate information to the press.

Historian Stephen White, in his book *Gorbachev and After*, credits Gorbachev with initiating enormous change that was clearly necessary to pull his people out of their economic doldrums and social miseries. What Gorbachev failed to see, says White, was that "a solution to the problems he had identified was likely to require a reconsideration of the basis of the Soviet system and not simply an attempt to manage that system more effectively."

Chronology

March 2, 1931	Born in the small peasant village of Privolnoye
September 1950	Enters Moscow State University
1954	Marries Raisa Titorenko at Moscow State University
1956	Returns home to become first secretary of the Stavropol city Komsomol organization
1963	Becomes chief of the agricultural department for the entire Stavropol region
1971	Is named to membership in the powerful Central Committee
November 1978	Joins the Kremlin's inner circle as agricultural secretary on the Secretariat of the Central Committee
March 11, 1985	Becomes leader of the Soviet Union after being elected general secretary of the Communist Party
May 1985	Tells U.S. secretary of commerce that it's "high time to defrost the potential for Soviet-American cooperation"
November 1985	Meets in Geneva with U.S. President Ronald Reagan
November 11, 1987	Accepts the forced resignation of Boris Yeltsin from the Moscow City Committee. Days later, hires Yeltsin as first deputy chairman of the State Committee for Construction
January 1, 1988	Begins policy of *perestroika*, or economic restructuring
February 1988	Completes withdrawal of Soviet troops from Afghanistan

May 25, 1989	Becomes president of the U.S.S.R.
August 19, 1991	Placed under house arrest by hard-line allies who attempt to overthrow the democratic reform movement
December 22, 1991	Eleven former republics agree to join Yeltsin's new commonwealth, ending the existence of the U.S.S.R.
December 25, 1991	Resigns as president of the now defunct U.S.S.R.

Further Reading

Kallen, Stuart A. *Gorbachev-Yeltsin: The Fall of Communism.* Edina, Minn.: Abdo and Daughters, 1992. Examines the events in the Soviet Union during the time of Gorbachev and Yeltsin, including the failed coup of 1991 and the collapse of the Soviet Union itself.

Kort, Michael. *Mikhail Gorbachev.* New York: Watts, 1990. Discusses the life of Gorbachev from his formative years to the present, and examines the reforms he introduced in the former Soviet Union.

Sproule, Anna. *Mikhail Gorbachev: Revolutionary for Democracy.* Milwaukee: Gareth Stevens Children's Books, 1991. An account of Gorbachev's role in the Soviet Union, as a leader who promoted a much freer way of life for the Russian people.

Czech playwright Vaclav Havel flashes the victory sign to several thousand Czechs from the balcony of Hradcany Castle the Friday after he was elected president of Czechoslovakia. (AP/Wide World Photos)

Vaclav Havel

Vaclav Havel's ascent from political dissident to the presidency of Czechoslovakia struck everyone, including himself, as improbable. But it happened in the final days of 1989. The leading light of the Czechoslovakian dissident movement and the hero of the Velvet Revolution maintains that he and his fellow revolutionaries never planned to be revolutionary dissidents. "We just happened to" become dissidents, he explained. "We don't know how. And we started landing in jails—now we also don't know how. We just did some things that seemed the decent things to do."

In hindsight, the journey seems almost to have been preordained. One thing led to another. Havel was a playwright whose works were banned, and so he became a political dissident who refused to be silenced. For this refusal, the activist spent nearly five years in prison. When Havel was finally freed, he was a revolutionary leading his country's peaceful transition—called the Velvet Revolution—from communism to democracy. With the old Communist regime gone, Havel was the overwhelming choice to be president. The playwright-activist became the first democratically elected president in the republic's 50-year history. Today he remains one of the world's most beloved heads of state.

Vaclav Havel was born in Prague, Czechoslovakia, on October 5, 1936, the first-born son of Vaclav M. and Bozena Vavreckova Havel. Havel's father was a wealthy man, a prominent real estate magnate and restaurateur in the commercial center of Prague. His father's brother owned the Barandov studios, the dominant motion picture company in Czechoslovakia. His grandfather had built the Lucerna Palace, the first steel-and-concrete building in Prague, an art nouveau masterpiece just off sprawling Wenceslas Square.

By all accounts Vasek, as he was known, was a polite and happy child who was friendly and good-natured though a bit clumsy and a touch shy. He had blond, curly hair, innocent blue eyes, and a boyish smile. He enjoyed painting, drawing, and reading everything he could get his hands on in the family's library. He became interested in poetry at a very young age.

But Vasek always felt a bit outside the mainstream because of his family's enormous wealth. They had a cook, a maid, even a chauffeur. His childhood was positively idyllic, even during Word War II. When a bomb damaged the family home in Prague on the banks of the Vltava, the Havel family simply moved to their country house in Moravia.

In 1948, Vasek's idyllic world was turned upside down. The Communists took power and confiscated his family's vast land holdings, including his father's restaurant and properties in Prague. Vasek was 12 years old, still a schoolboy, as he watched his very wealthy family being forced into the margins of society.

For a short time his father was imprisoned, though he would later be released and find work as an office clerk at Lucerna, the very same complex he had once owned. Vasek's mother became a tour guide. For his once-wealthy parents, the hard times would never really end. The family had a difficult life, having lost all their holdings, but they would bravely bear it together.

Havel had graduated from the district grammar school a year before the Communist takeover, and his mother decided that now he should leave home and experience life on his own at a boarding school. She sent him to the prestigious Academy of King George of Podebrady, a prep school modeled on English boarding schools. Havel spent three years there. The final year he was there, his brother Ivan also attended. But Havel was forced to return home to Prague after his third year at Podebrady. This was a consequence of his family's "bourgeois" history. Because Havel had been born into the bourgeoisie, he was not to be allowed easy access to an education.

By day Havel worked in a chemical plant in Prague, washing test tubes, and at night he took classes at a local high school. His opportunity for a formal higher education was bleak, and in his spare time he combed his father's bookshelves. With friends his own age at night school—all born in 1936—he founded an intellectual circle or literary group, the "Thirty-sixers." The group gathered at Prague's Café Slavia, where they swapped poetry and gossip and mingled with the older writers they idolized. The group held symposia and even published a typewritten magazine. Mostly they debated heatedly, for hours upon hours, the hidden treasures of Czech literature and history.

A defiant new underground was growing in Prague, and Havel was at its center. Havel and most of his friends in and out of the Thirty-sixers were becoming ideological renegades within the Communist system. Havel's father did not oppose his son's radicalism. But because everyone else in the family had been engineers, he was surprised at his son's continuing interest in poetry. One day Havel's father arranged for his son to visit the lyric poet Jaroslav Seifert. Havel brought his own early attempts at writing poetry for Seifert to see. This visit was the first of many Havel would pay to the great Czech poet.

It was a great disappointment to Havel that he was not allowed to attend the Academy of Performing Arts. He stubbornly applied many times, but the Communist regime in Prague had set strict guidelines. If one's parents had not chosen to join the Communist Party, it was virtually impossible to gain admittance. But having many friends at the academy, Havel managed to see many of the foreign films that did not reach the public movie houses. Although the films were officially forbidden, government officials did not bother to crack down on those who watched them. Only much later did it dawn on the Communists that the Western films were affecting the thinking of Czechs.

In the spring of 1955, he met a student named Olga Splichalova. Olga wanted to be an actress. She seemed the perfect match for a budding playwright. At the café they shared their dreams. Olga was a peasant from Zizkov who had grown up on the streets. She had once supported herself and her sister's children operating a stocking-mending machine, but in a sewing accident she had lost several of her fingertips. Now she was eking out a living as an usher at Prague's Theater on the Balustrade.

Havel's upper-class parents frowned on the relationship. They thought Olga too forceful and outspoken. When the couple married 10 years later, they sent out wedding invitations declaring that they were already married. The only people present at their ceremony were two witnesses. The couple had no children, but Olga would prove to be the best partner a dissident could have. With her husband she would tough it out through all the arrests and the police surveillance. She also tolerated her husband's frequent infidelities.

Before marrying, though, Havel had had critical essays published in a theater magazine, beginning when he was only 19. The most important of these was a monograph on the Czech writer and painter Josef Capek. For some time Havel was torn between theater and fiction, but finally he made up his mind. "Drama for me is the better genre," he said, "not novels or short stories." He did continue to write some poems, however, in addition to his plays and occasional essays.

Coming into his own as a writer, Havel was greatly influenced by the works of such officially forbidden avant-garde authors as Kafka, Beckett, and Ionesco. Typically in Havel's writings the world is in such a miserable state that it can only get better. The system is usually collapsing, but its leaders still believe it works. Everyone knows that the emperor wears no clothes, but people allow the system to go on because they are used to the problems.

Havel's writing career was sidetracked when he registered at the Czechoslovak University of Technology in Prague. He'd done so because he was afraid of being drafted into compulsory military service. He was accepted in the university's Department of Public Transport. Havel initially thought that he would enter the Academy of Performing Arts later, but in 1957 he was forced into the army. By this time, however, he had already begun to make his mark publicly.

The year before, he had delivered a memorable address at a meeting of young writers loyal to the Communist regime. At the so-called House of Writers, the blond young man with clear blue eyes looked like an innocent boy when he appeared at the podium. Then he lashed out at his fellow writers for their hypocrisy. Havel talked about the suppression of literature and of those who were blackballed from publishing. He warned the Communists of the coming of a new generation of writers who would speak the truth.

Within days of his 21st birthday, Havel was off to military service for two years. When he boarded a train for Ceke Budejovice, a tearful Olga stood on the platform. Havel served as a tank commander, which was considered an honor, but he couldn't get the theater out of his system. With the help of a close friend, Havel formed a theater company in the service. In his first performance, in a play called *September Nights*, Havel played the villain, a Communist official. He played his part so convincingly that the troop commander suspected he was showing his true anti-Communist feelings.

Havel was soon relieved of his duties as a tank commander. He was not in the least disappointed. Later he would say that the punishment only spared him from having to drag a bazooka with him during training exercises. Havel turned to writing his own plays. He saw his trips to theater competitions as a pleasant respite from his military duties. One of his dramas, about the problems of military life, went a little overboard. Havel was branded as antimilitary when he performed the one-man play during an all-army review. The play was condemned and the matter hushed up, but Havel received no official punishment.

On finishing his military service in the late 1950s, Havel supported himself for a year as a stagehand before joining the Theater on the Balustrade, an avant-garde group founded in 1958. Starting as a stagehand and electrician for the group, he went on to become dramaturge, or literary manager, and finally resident playwright. The Theater on the Balustrade would become the leading dramatic ensemble in Prague, and Havel was its fastest-rising star.

Havel's reputation as a great playwright exploded like a supernova with the success of his first solo play, *The Garden Party*. In the four-act play, set in the Prague of 1963, the protagonist is an ambitious young man who is a sort of idiot savant, good at two things: playing chess and parroting political buzzwords and platitudes. He is so brilliant in his mimicry of officialese that he rises quickly in the government. The play clearly showed Havel's disdain for the Communist system.

Meanwhile Havel had already begun writing his best-known and most frequently performed play, *The Memorandum*. Begun in 1960, it was five years in the writing and did not receive a production at the Theater on the Balustrade until 1965. His next major work at the Balustrade was *The Increased Difficulty of Concentration.* Produced in April of 1968, it went beyond satirizing totalitarian bureaucracies. Havel was making comments about the universal themes of alienation and loss of communication. Havel's plot structure underscored the dreadful nausea of life under communism, through events that played back and forth, like a film on rewind. Again, Havel's writing revealed his deep-seated antipathy for totalitarianism.

Havel's passport had been confiscated, and he had been unable to travel abroad prior to the reforms introduced by the new Communist Party chief, Alexander Dubcek. During this reform period, known as the Prague Spring of 1968, Havel visited the United States. The occasion was the first American production of *The Memorandum*, by Joseph Papp's Public Theater in New York City. The trip meant a great deal to him, since he longed to see the products of his labors produced on the American stage.

The freedoms of 1968 were short-lived. Alarmed at the course of events under Dubcek, the Soviet Union, along with other Warsaw Pact countries, crushed the Prague Spring. As tanks rolled into Czechoslovakia in August of 1968, Havel rushed to an underground radio station monitored by Radio Free Europe in Munich. At the microphone he pleaded for Western intellectuals to come to the aid of his country "in the name of all Czech and Slovak writers."

Havel also addressed groups of Czech artists and workers, urging them to unite in the cause of human rights. In doing so he attracted a dedicated group of theater people and others committed to protesting repression. For this rebellion, Havel would pay a heavy price. After the reform movement was crushed that August, his work was banned by the hard-line regime that replaced the reform government of Dubcek.

The period following the Soviet invasion of 1968 was a dark time for everyone in Czechoslovakia. For Havel personally, it was horrendously bleak. Though he continued to write, the government banned his plays and writings altogether. His manuscripts were circulated privately and produced in Western Europe. Havel's passport was permanently withdrawn and he was repeatedly arrested during the 1970s. He found that there were fewer and fewer dependable friends. Some had emigrated. Others were so afraid of being seen with him that they took to avoiding him on the street. The manager of the Balustrade even barred him from entering the theater.

Since there was nothing worth seeing in the theaters anyway, Havel went out less often. He and Olga bought a cottage in the northern Bohemian town of Hradecek. Their modest little home became a meeting place for dissident writers and reform-minded Communists from the Prague Spring era who had been kicked out of the party. Eventually, Havel and this group began to consider themselves dissidents.

Havel and Olga lived in Hradecek for the remainder of the year, gathering for days at a time with other dissidents. But soon Havel was forced into menial work stacking barrels in a brewery in Trutnov. This was not for money. His plays were now meeting with great success abroad. He could have easily lived off his royalties. But because he was not recognized as a writer within Czechoslovakia, he needed to have official employment or risk charges of parasitism.

In a few months, however, Havel knew almost everything about barrels of beer. He learned how the barrels were manufactured, who made the iron hoops attached to them, what was put in them, and just about everything there was to know about the world of brewing. But he was merely putting a very good face on his radically downgraded lifestyle. Deep down what bothered him most was the shift away from creativity in Czech society.

His response to this crisis took the form of two satires written in the early 1970s. His first effort, *The Conspirators*, portrayed the history of the Communists as static and unchanging. The second, *The Mountain Hotel*, was set in a windowless madhouse. It seemed clear that Havel himself was suffering from his isolation. In the next few years he returned to realism, with plays that pitted dissident artists against conformists.

Following an amateur production of Havel's adaptation of the *The Beggar's Opera* in 1975, even members of the audience became subject to police reprisal. Havel had had enough. He took aim at the highest levels of the Communist regime, hurling charges directly at First Party Secretary Gustav Husak. "Society can be enriched and cultivated only through self-knowledge," Havel wrote in an open letter to Husak. "And the main instrument of society's self-knowledge is its culture. Where total control over society is sought, the first thing to be suppressed is its culture."

It was a scorching analysis of the brutal dictatorship. Sending the letter struck many of Havel's friends as a virtual act of suicide. Strangely, Husak did nothing in reaction. The regime seemed hesitant, somehow—cowed, perhaps, by Havel's special status as an internationally acclaimed playwright. Copies of his letter were circulated widely. Havel later said that "it was read by practically everyone who still cared."

The effect of Havel's open letter was to galvanize at least 273 other Czech dissidents into forming an opposition group called Charter 77. Founded early in 1977, The Charter, as it came to be known, protested the failure of the Czechoslovak authorities to honor the Helsinki accords on human rights. In the eyes of the regime, however, Havel had finally crossed the line. The response from the government was swift and predictable. A wave of arrests of Charter 77 signatories followed, accompanied by an official statement from the government that "freedom of expression" had to be "consistent with the interests of the working people."

Havel was among the first to be arrested. As one of the principal Charter 77 spokesmen, he remained in jail for four months. The charge: subversion of the republic. At his trial, a one-sided kangaroo court, the prosecutor cited the evidence. It was the banned writings Havel had sent out of the country for publication abroad. Havel was found guilty but released from prison with a 14-month suspended sentence.

Toward the end of the 1970s, he was watched constantly by government authorities. Agents of the secret police were always stationed at the door of his second-floor apartment. A state security car was permanently parked on the dead-end street outside his apartment house. Nevertheless, Charter 77 managed to survive as the longest-lived human rights group in Eastern Europe.

By March of 1979 Havel was virtually under house arrest. On May 29, government officials seized Havel at his apartment in Prague and imprisoned him without a trial. Then, on July 22, Havel's father died. His son had been in prison for two months when, to everyone's great surprise, his jailers brought him to his father's funeral. Nothing like this had ever happened before in Czechoslovakia. Havel was returned to prison immediately following the funeral. In mid-August, he was offered a chance to travel to the United States, but he turned down the opportunity to defect. Havel said he was not going to change his life and drop his political activity because of a few years spent in prison.

The trial that followed in October was the most important political trial in Czechoslovakia since the 1950s. In the mornings, before the proceedings began, Havel's friends and sympathizers would gather outside the courthouse, but none was let inside the building. Havel was convicted along with six other dissidents by the Prague People's Court on charges of "subversion" and contacts "with a foreign agent." He was sentenced to four and a half years of hard labor at Hermanice prison.

In prison Havel turned again to writing for solace. His brother Ivan's letters inspired him, posing philosophical questions for Havel to answer. Ivan never wrote of his own life or problems. Havel did not know, for instance, that at one point in 1981 Ivan and Olga spent four days in jail, allegedly for bringing banned literature across the border. On this occasion all three Havels were in jail simultaneously. Vaclav Havel, still in prison, later told Olga he'd just as soon emigrate if the two of them were ever in prison again. When she assured him they'd never emigrate, a stone seemed to have been lifted from his heart.

By 1983 Havel's health had begun to fail. He fell seriously ill with pneumonia complicated by a lung abscess. Following an urgent appeal from the international human rights community, his sentence was suspended in February 1983, a few months short of its completion.

A long convalescence at the cottage at Hradecek kept the tired activist from writing another play. It was not until a year after his release that he was able to write a full-length play. When he finally sat down to write *Largo Desolato*, he finished it in record time. The play, which concerns an author who returns home from prison, is perhaps Havel's best and certainly his most autobiographical work.

Though released from prison, Havel continued to be harassed by the authorities. One day in August of 1984, just after he'd sent out *Largo Desolato*, the state security police barged into his cottage. Without a search warrant, they ransacked his house, taking away books, letters, magazines, photographs and cassette tapes. On a trip across Czechoslovakia the following year, he was stopped and taken into custody for 24 hours on two separate occasions.

Returning to Hradecek, Havel threw himself into his next piece of work, *Temptation*, a 10-act play that he wrote in just 10 days. It was an unsettling Faustian drama about a Czech coward who offers everything to the devil. On finishing it, the drained writer collapsed from exhaustion. Gradually he was finding less and less time for writing. The leading light of the Czechoslovakian opposition movement was being tugged further and further into politics. He was meeting foreign ministers and other dignitaries from the West who liked to keep in touch with prominent opposition figures in Eastern Europe.

By the summer of 1988, Prague was heating up. On August 21, 1988, the 20th anniversary of the Soviet invasion of Czechoslovakia, riot police attacked demonstrators in the streets of Prague. In the ensuing months, tension spread and intensified every day. In October the police searched Havel's apartment and his cottage at Hradecek. In addition to many books and writings, his computer was seized. Havel was not home at the time, but the police hunted him down that night and held him at Ruzyne prison until the end of the month.

The government was now growing increasingly concerned about rising tensions among the dissident population. The more the authorities pretended that they were following the path of democratization that was taking place in the Soviet Union under Mikhail Gorbachev, the more the protesters criticized the Czech government. Meanwhile, *glasnost* was clearly transforming cultural and social life in the Soviet Union. By the late 1980s all of Czechoslovakia began to realize that Gorbachev would never send troops to shore up the Communist government in Prague, as the Soviet Union had in 1968.

Yet the situation was slightly different now in Czechoslovakia. Ever since the Soviet invasion of 1968 put an end to the Prague Spring experiment, Czechoslovakia had been governed by one of the most repressive regimes in Eastern

Europe. Lulled by a higher standard of living than most other Soviet bloc nations, many Czechoslovaks had passively accepted a totalitarian way of life.

Throughout Eastern Europe, 1989 was a banner year, though it opened inauspiciously for Havel and his repressed countrymen. In January he was arrested for the crime of placing flowers on a memorial to the Prague Spring martyr Jan Palach. Havel was sentenced to nine months in prison—a big mistake on the part of the Communist authorities, for it soon became clear that Havel's arrest was uniting the broadly based opposition.

A public campaign for the release of Havel took off with surprising force and speed. By March, 1,000 intellectuals had signed a letter demanding his release. The appeal was rejected by the government, but Havel's sentence was reduced. By May 17, he was home again, set free on condition that he was not to engage in political activity.

Havel seemed incapable of forsaking politics. He drafted a petition of dissident demands, entitled "Just a Few Sentences," condemning the hypocrisy of the Czechoslovak leadership for resisting democracy while proclaiming "restructuring" and "democratization." "Just a Few Sentences" recalled a famous "Two Thousand Words" reformist document of the 1968 Prague Spring led by Alexander Dubcek. Though that experiment with democracy failed miserably, more than 20 years later it still inspired a generation of reformers who, like Havel, had come of age in the 1960s. "Just a Few Sentences" was circulated among dissidents, students, workers, and even members of the Communist Party who were willing to take a political stand. Eventually, the petition was signed by some 40,000 people who represented the whole spectrum of society.

For months the country's leaders had watched in tense silence as communism fell in Poland, Hungary, and finally East Germany. Soviet leader Mikhail Gorbachev's tacit acceptance of these revolutions inspired ordinary Czechoslovaks to take to the streets to demand their freedoms. On November 17, 1989, 25,000 Czech students marched through Prague. When riot police closed in and beat them, the violence only inflamed the students.

A strike was called, and on the following day many people saw Havel for the first time at the podium of the Realistic Theater. A group called the Civic Forum was formed at the theater that day. And thus began Czechoslovakia's peaceful Velvet Revolution.

In his speech, Havel declared that anyone who felt he was a member of Civic Forum was a member. He demanded the immediate resignation of President Husak, Communist Party leader Milos Jakes, and other officials. He also demanded an investigation of the November 17 police action against student protesters, and called for the release of prisoners of conscience.

On November 19, an evening meeting was arranged between the Civic Forum and government officials. But Prime Minister Ladislas Adamec stubbornly refused to attend the meeting if Vaclav Havel was also in attendance. An unbending ideologist, Adamec just didn't see that opposition to his government had reached a boiling point. Right outside Adamec's window Wenceslas Square was filling up with protesters who saw Havel as their undisputed leader. A nervous excitement filled the air. It was a rare moment of accelerated change. The regime's days seemed numbered.

More than 300,000 people swarmed into Wenceslas Square. By Friday, half a million people—nearly a third of the city's population—turned out for demonstrations. They poured into the square through the narrow streets of Prague, snarling the traffic and filling the air with chants and cheers. They lit thousands of candles for those who had been beaten the week before. "Jakes, Jakes, Jakes!" they shouted. "Your time is up!"

Finally, on November 24, Jakes convened an emergency meeting of the Central Committee. It was there that Jakes, along with the entire Politburo, resigned. Upon hearing the news, crowds exploded in jubilant celebrations. Reformers danced in the square. After so many decades without freedom, it seemed unreal to the Czech people that major changes could occur so quickly. It was as if Havel had written an absurdist play, ending with a stunning victory for an opposition group that, only a week before, had barely counted as a political force.

The excitement took over all of Czechoslovakia, crossing all social boundaries. In Wenceslas Square, elderly pensioners mixed easily with long-haired students and beefy steelworkers. Groups of people gathered on street corners to debate the future. People placed flickering candles on the steps of subways and in windows. They draped in banners, flags, and photos a statue of King Wenceslas that stood at the rallying point at the top of Wenceslas Square.

The celebrations that broke out following the old guard's resignation were dampened when a new Communist Party leader, Zdenek Urbanek, was appointed by the Central Committee. He was widely regarded as another hard-liner. And Wednesday, December 2, more than 500,000 people braved bitter cold to gather outside a huge sports stadium to hear Havel speak about the country's political future. The dissident playwright, who had so often been jailed for his outspoken liberalism, continued to place pressure on the new regime. "Power now goes once again to the neo-Stalinists," he declared. "We are not satisfied."

"Beginning tomorrow, we must start a dialogue with the authorities."

Dramatic political events continued to occur throughout the month of December. Loudspeakers were erected at a mass protest on December 4 on Wenceslas Square. A publishing house allowed Civic Forum to use its balcony. It was a bitterly cold December day, yet the Square was so crowded that it was impossible to move without bumping into someone. Practically all of Prague had braved the chill to hear Havel speak the truth about Civic Forum and the Communist dictatorship.

Havel addressed the crowd from a balcony overlooking a vast sea of protesters on Wenceslas Square. The huge crowd hung on his every word. They responded to his speech with triumphant democratic slogans. How refreshing it was for them to hear the truth blasting from the balcony. A television studio broadcast the demonstration live, interrupting it every so often with music from rock bands. A popular singer who had been banned for 19 years sang the Czechoslovakian national anthem.

"Beginning tomorrow," Havel said, "we must start a dialogue with the authorities." Everywhere in the streets were posters that read, "Put Havel in the Castle," a reference to the medieval Hradcany Castle that had been the traditional seat of power in Czechoslovakia. At the end of the demonstration the people in the square made an extraordinary spontaneous gesture. They all took their keys out of their pockets and began shaking them. Three hundred thousand jangling key rings, symbolizing the keys to the castle, sounded like massive bells declaring a death knell for the Communist government.

Finally Prime Minister Adamec caved in and agreed to meet with Havel. On December 28, in a meeting with government authorities, Havel negotiated an end to the Communist Party's 41-year monopoly on power. Government leaders announced that non-Communists would be included in a new cabinet. The regime also agreed to grant

President Vaclav Havel with Prime Minister Margaret Thatcher of Great Britain. (UPP/Photoreporters, Inc.)

the opposition free access to the media, eliminate mandatory Marxist-Leninist university instruction, release all political prisoners, and form a commission to examine the November 19 beating of protesters.

The following Monday, Adamec resigned. As the main opposition party, Civic Forum would govern in a new coalition with the government. The only argument was over who should become president. Havel at first was reluctant to take the job. He had seen himself as the conscience of the nation, not as its ruler. "I am a playwright," he said, "not a President."

The demands from the streets were clear. The people wanted Havel. He decided that he would serve for an interim period, until federal elections in the summer of 1990. On December 29, 1989, Havel was elected to the post of interim president. Just seven months out of jail, he became Czechoslovakia's first democratically-elected non-Communist president in more than 40 years. The vote in the Czechoslovakian parliament, the Federal Assembly, was unanimous. Czechoslovakia had finally had its peaceful "revolution from below." Havel's first address to the nation as president was magnificent. "People," he shouted, "your government has returned to you."

As a playwright, Havel seemed an unlikely president, yet he was so clearly the leader of the dissident community that it seemed no else could have taken power in postrevolutionary Czechoslovakia. Immediately he became preoccupied with the difficult task of guiding Czechoslovakia's return to democracy.

Havel set up his government in Prague's Hradcany Castle. A scooter was given to Havel by Czechoslovakian-born tennis star Martina Navratilova to speed his trips through the castle's lengthy corridors. His administration was filled with people who had come of age with him during the Prague Spring. Havel received a steady stream of foreign rock-star dignitaries such as the Rolling Stones, Lou Reed, and Frank Zappa. The latter was made an official in the new government's Ministry of Culture.

Amid the giddy euphoria, Havel was facing obstacles that no dissident, no matter how celebrated, had ever had to face. Foremost were the inevitable problems of establishing capitalism. Prices doubled and tripled when controls were lifted in January 1990. Unemployment soared. Havel had never professed any economic expertise, and some of his programs, like his cherished dream

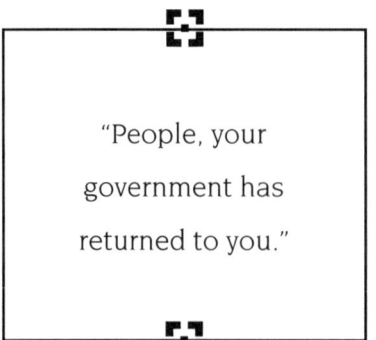

"People, your government has returned to you."

of weaning Czechoslovakia from the armaments industry, had to be deferred in the wake of vociferous public protests.

It was unsettling for Havel to be thrust into a position where decisions have more to do with nuances of policy than with the stark contrast between good and evil. After years of inhabiting a black-and-white world, he faced all the ambiguous shades of gray. Meanwhile, capitalism ushered in a gap in the earning power between Czechs and Slovaks that communism had kept a lid on. Havel had always believed that for the citizens of both the Czech and Slovak Republics it was more advantageous to live in a collective state. But the gap kept widening until Slovak separatists started rioting. For the first time, there were anti-Havel demonstrations, especially in Slovakia, where Havel came close to being assaulted by an angry separatist mob.

Havel was reelected to the presidency in July 1990. But his vision of "an intellectual, cultural and really human state" had already come face to face with stark reality. He tried to reform the Constitution in 1991 but failed. He also was unable to prevent a nationwide witch-hunt for Communist collaborators, and he watched from the sidelines as the Civic Forum Party fell apart. Free Czechoslovakia, he said, "behaves worse than when it was in chains." Havel was clearly frustrated, and he saw that true democracy could not be established overnight.

With few concrete powers as president, there was less and less he could do to counter Slovak separatism. In July of 1992 he left the castle, his resignation from the presidency prompted by the failure of his efforts to avert a split between the Czechs and the Slovaks. The majority of the population of the Slovak Republic had been pushing for separation, and it was clear that the two economies could not live side by side. The Slovaks favored a policy of slowing and limiting reform, and so the division of the state became a necessary operation. The split became official on January 1, following a vote by Slovaks. The following month the parliament of the Czech Republic elected him president of the new country, sending him back to the castle.

Today Havel remains one of the most beloved heads of state in the world. He will always be remembered for presiding over one of the smoother transitions in post-Communist Central Europe. The Czechs continue to adore him, despite their many problems, because his moral influence remains so strong. In large part, this is because Havel is not wedded to power like so many other politicians. He has often said: "The interests of my country are more important to me than staying in power. I don't feel that I am a person enchanted by power, someone who longs for power, who wants to hold any office. The point is that I want to work for something, that I cherish some values, that I want to continue this struggle or work."

Havel's life is a testament to the price a person will pay to achieve freedom under extreme circumstances. The price was heavy. Havel endured long imprisonment and hard labor that severely affected his career as a playwright. But his political ideals are no greater than his literary ambitions. For Havel, politics could not be separated from literature. In the end, he achieved tremendous success as a writer and a politician. He compromised nothing, and achieved everything.

According to Michael T. Kaufman, author of *The Collapse of*

"The interests of my country are more important to me than staying in power. I don't feel that I am a person enchanted by power, someone who longs for power, who wants to hold any office. The point is that I want to work for something, that I cherish some values, that I want to continue this struggle or work."

Communism, Havel "is as eligible a candidate for secular sainthood as anyone who comes to mind. Mr. Havel had a vision, he kept the faith, he lived and told the truth, he endured pain and isolation, and eventually he and his views of democracy and pluralism triumphed gloriously."

Chronology

October 5, 1936	Born in Prague
Spring 1955	Meets Olga Splichalova, whom he marries 10 years later
1955	Publishes his first critical essay
1956	Delivers critical address at the House of Writers
October 1957	Conscripted into military service for two years
1963	First solo play, *The Garden Party*, is produced at the Theater on the Balustrade
April 1968	*The Increased Difficulty of Concentration* is produced at the Theater on the Balustrade
Spring 1968	Amid short-lived flowering of democratic reform known as the Prague Spring, travels abroad to see the first American production of *The Memorandum*, in New York City
August 20, 1968	Soviet Union invades Czechoslovakia and crushes the Prague Spring
1975	Publishes an open letter critical of Communist Party. The letter galvanizes 273 other Czech dissidents into forming an opposition group called Charter 77

1977	Jailed for four months after founding Charter 77 group protesting the failure of the government to honor the Helsinki accords on human rights
March 1979	Placed under house arrest
May 29, 1979	Arrested and jailed for four years, during which time he writes "Letters to Olga"
February 1983	Released from prison four months short of completing his sentence
August 21, 1988	On the 20th anniversary of the Soviet invasion of Czechoslovakia, riot police attack demonstrators in the streets of Prague
January 1989	Arrested for placing flowers on a memorial to the Prague Spring martyr Jan Palach
May 17, 1989	Released from prison one month early after 1,000 intellectuals sign a letter demanding his release
November 19, 1989	Forms Civic Forum and calls for the release of prisoners of conscience
November 24, 1989	President Milos Jakes resigns along with the entire Politburo
December 28, 1989	Negotiates an end to the Communist Party's 41-year-old monopoly on power
December 29, 1989	Elected interim president
July 1990	Reelected to the presidency
July 1992	Resigns as president after failure to avert split between the Czechs and Slovaks
February 1993	Elected president of the Czech Republic

Further Reading

Kriseova, Eda. *Vaclav Havel: The Authorized Biography.* New York: St. Martin's Press, 1993. Portrays Havel as the conscience of his nation, a stubborn man with high moral principles and one of the great political thinkers of the 20th century.

Simmons, Michael. *The Reluctant President.* London: Methuen, 1991. Focuses on the political life of Havel, with emphasis on the events leading to the Velvet Revolution and the collapse of Communism in Czechoslovakia.

Symynkwicz, Jeffrey. *Vaclav Havel and the Velvet Revolution.* Newark, N.J.: Dillon Press, 1995. Concentrates on the personality of Havel as the one genuine hero of the Velvet Revolution.

On December 22, 1990, Lech Walesa celebrates his inauguration as president of Poland. (St. Petersburg Press)

Lech Walesa

In 1980, when an unemployed electrician named Lech Walesa scaled the fence at the Lenin Shipyard in Gdansk, Poland, it was a singular act of defiance that galvanized opposition to Poland's Communist regime. At the time, labor unrest had erupted into massive strikes and Walesa was known to the authorities only as an incorrigible troublemaker. A mere three months later, as the organizer and leader of the Solidarity Free Trade Union, the only independent trade union in the Communist world, Walesa was catapulted to international fame.

Nine years later, Solidarity—or "unity" among Polish workers—forced the government to hold the country's first truly free elections in more than 40 years. Walesa, hailed as the savior of a free Poland, was elected president. By speaking the simple language of the working man, in 10 years the portly shipyard worker with a mustache and impish brown eyes had risen from the rank and file of workers to the presidency of Poland. And by balancing militancy and moderation, Walesa succeeded in satisfying the basic demands of Poland's aroused workers without provoking intervention by the Soviet Union. He had pulled off one of the most skillful tightrope acts in history.

When Leszek Michael Walesa was born on September 29, 1943, in the village of Popowo, Poland, his father was in a Nazi concentration camp. His father's arrest had come without any warning one dark night during the German occupation of Poland during World War II. Some Nazis had come for his father's brother, who had escaped from a German concentration camp and was hiding in a nearby forest. Since they could not find Walesa's uncle, the Germans took Lech's father away on horseback to a prison camp at Mlyniec. Many of the young men from the surrounding villages were executed there, but Lech's father managed to survive the war and come home—only to die two months later of illness and exhaustion.

Before these tragedies occurred, Lech's father had made the most of his small peasant farm near the Vistula River north of Warsaw. When he married Feliksa Kaminska, he knew that more money would be needed to raise his growing family. Additional income from building houses and sheds had helped to make ends meet. His father's death left Lech's poor mother with four hungry mouths to feed: Izabela, Edward, Stanislaw, and Lech, the youngest. The 27-year-old widow had only a small plot of land, but her brother-in-law had promised her husband on his deathbed that he would marry the widow and provide for her children.

Lech and his two brothers and sister never warmed up to their Uncle Stanislaw Walesa, now their stepfather. They found it hard to accept that their mother had married him only because she didn't want to live alone. Besides, he was strict and argued often with their mother. Lech would interrupt them frequently and plead with them to stop bickering. He'd ask them to "sit down, think carefully, and explain your arguments without getting worked up." Lech was learning very early the value of negotiation.

Lech was too young to remember much of World War II. He grew up with full knowledge of the horror Adolf Hitler had inflicted upon the Polish people. He knew his father had died protecting Lech's uncle. Though country life formed his character, Lech didn't like it very much. As he became aware of the world in the late 1940s, he was a child learning the hard way how much labor it takes for a peasant family to survive on one small plot of land.

After the war, young Lech attended a nearby school that was run by the Roman Catholic Church until it was taken over by the Soviet-controlled Communist Party in 1952. Communist history lessons completely distorted the truth about Polish history. But Lech knew the truth from what his family had told him, and he usually told his teachers what he thought. Later he would become well known for his outspokenness.

In addition to doing his school work, Lech tended geese, took the cows out to pasture, and did a variety of manual jobs. During the summers he worked at a brickyard to bring in extra money for the family. He grew up respecting hard work but also rebelling against it. All that hard work never seemed to improve the quality of his family's life. Whenever he complained, however, his stern stepfather beat him with a belt.

Despite the grim realities of daily life, Lech and his schoolmates managed to have some fun in their spare time. In the summer, they used to rush to the edge of a nearby lake, fling themselves into the water, and swim out as far as possible. They played soccer with a ball made of rags and stuffed with horsehair. In the winter they'd go out on the ice, jumping from one piece to another.

Like most Poles, the family was Roman Catholic, and the Walesas were a deeply religious family. They said their daily prayers morning, afternoon, and evening. Each Sunday young Lech would make the four-mile trek with his family along a dusty country road to the nearest Catholic church. His old, tight-fitting shoes gave him blisters, and some days he was in tears by the time he reached church.

Lech was good at math and physics. It was this technical aptitude that led him to train as an electrician. Though he was qualified to attend the College of Technology, his parents could not afford to send him there. Lech's mother desperately wanted one of her children to become a priest. Lech was the one son she thought would take his vows. He thought so too, until he discovered girls. At that point he decided against the celibate life of a Roman Catholic priest.

In 1959 he left home for a state vocational school in nearby Lipno. When he left he made up his mind to abandon farm work forever. "You never knew," he wrote, "whether something would grow or whether it would be eaten up by insects or pecked up by birds." With his stocky build, Walesa was known as a bit of a bully, but a likable one, at vocational school. He laughed easily and delighted in playing practical jokes. After graduating he was hired as an electrician in the state agricultural department for a brief period until he was drafted into the army. It was in the army that Walesa grew his trademark bushy mustache.

When he got out of the army, in 1967, many young people from his village had begun to emigrate to the cities. Walesa became one of them. He moved to the Baltic seaport of Gdansk and found a job as an electrician in the sprawling Lenin Shipyard. Despite its stunning Gothic churches, Gdansk had dilapidated houses, grimy factories, and potholed streets. However, there was a little flower shop that brought joy to Walesa's life. While stopping there one day to get some change, he was quite taken with the florist's assistant, Danuta Golos. He returned later to ask her for a date.

Like Walesa, Golos had grown up on a farm but decided to leave it for the excitement of the city. The couple fell in love and on November 8, 1969, they were married. They started married life in a rented room in Gdansk, where they stayed only four months. From there they moved into the attic of a private apartment above a beauty shop. They had a single room and a kitchen, but at least they had it all to themselves.

After a year the young family moved with their first-born child, baby Bogdan, to a worker's hotel. Living there was unbearable, however, because of the constant fighting and drunken rowdiness of the other tenants. Finally, when Lech found a two-room apartment, the couple could breathe a little. Lech's growing family made him work harder than ever. He was popular among his fellow workers and was a natural leader. Soon he became a job inspector, a position that taught him a lot about the working conditions at the shipyard.

The workers trusted Walesa to speak out for them. As Christmas approached in 1970, Walesa began marching in the streets with his workers for the first time, demanding higher wages and better working conditions. During the violent "bread riots" in protest of increases in the price of food, the government called out the police to crush the demonstrations. More than 100 demonstrators were killed in the streets in the crackdown. Ultimately, the bloodshed produced nothing but broken promises from the government.

Six years later, when Edward Gierek, the first secretary of the Polish Communist Party, attempted to end the five-year freeze on meat and other food prices, worker discontent again erupted in strikes and violent demonstrations. Walesa joined the strike committee that briefly shut down the shipyard. To avert escalation of the crisis, Gierek quickly restored the freeze on prices. Walesa was dismissed from his electrician's job at the shipyard for his involvement with the strike committee.

Dismissing Walesa from his job would prove to be a fatal tactical blunder for the government. The unemployed electrician had been punished, but his determination had not dulled. He used his dismissal as an opportunity to become a full-time agitator. By now a father of eight, he lived inconspicuously, providing for his large family as best he could despite successive job losses and jailings for labor agitation.

Walesa was strongly influenced by his contact with the radical Committee for Social Self-Defense (KOR), although by comparison he was a moderate. KOR had been founded by dissident intellectuals to provide medical, legal, and material aid for workers who, like Walesa, were fired, jailed or under attack for having taken part in strikes and demonstrations.

Walesa began to help edit and distribute an underground bimonthly newspaper, *The Coastal Worker*, "the organ of the founding committee of the free trade unions." The union was established, with Walesa's help, in April 1978. By January 1979, the first issue of *The Coastal Worker* boldly proclaimed the beginning of what became known as the illegal Baltic Committee for Free and Independent Trade Unions.

The following July, Walesa was one of many to sign a charter of workers' rights published in *The Coastal Worker*—a charter of which he was one of the principal authors. Walesa's most important statement in the charter was the demand for the right to free trade unions. "Strikes are useful short-term weapons," he wrote, "but free and independent trade unions are necessary to ensure that the gains won through a strike are not later lost. Only they will give us an equal footing in negotiations, a power the authorities cannot ignore."

> "Strikes are useful short-term weapons, but free and independent trade unions are necessary to ensure that the gains won through a strike are not later lost. Only they will give us an equal footing in negotiations, a power the authorities cannot ignore."

Although the gravelly-voiced activist was not a powerful speaker, he had a direct, low-key style that appealed to his audiences, as did his mixing of nationalism with religion. A crucifix was displayed wherever he spoke and he always wore a medallion of the Black Madonna of Czestochowa—to Poles a symbol of the Virgin Mary and her spiritual renewal of the country's predominantly Roman Catholic people. Since Poland had been reduced to little more than a colony of the Soviet Union, Walesa's proud display of the medallion on his lapel was his own statement against the officially atheist Communist state.

Life seemed bleak for the unemployed father of eight trying to wriggle out from under the weight of a totalitarian system. But Walesa's progress as a labor leader in the late seventies was bolstered when in October of 1978 Cardinal Karol Wojtyla of Poland became the first Slavic pope in the history of the Roman Catholic Church. It was a major event for Poland. When Wojtyla, now known as Pope John Paul II, returned to his native country in 1979 for a remarkable nine-day visit, the demoralized Polish people seemed to come together in a renewal of national spirit.

The following year, 1980, the Polish government doubled meat prices and set in motion a chain of events that would make Lech Walesa a household name. Workers demanded higher wages to compensate for the increased prices, but the government refused to comply. On July 1 laborers in factories throughout Poland stopped working. In August, at the Lenin Shipyard in Gdansk, the workers went on strike. Among their demands was the immediate reinstatement of Walesa and two other dismissed workers. The first thing the Gdansk workers did was affix a cross, an image of the Virgin Mary, and a portrait of John Paul II on the gates of the shipyard.

Walesa approached the gates of the shipyard as television crews from around the world videotaped him. In the dark of night, with the world watching the scene on television, he scaled the fence and joined the cheering workers occupying the shipyard. It was one of the most singularly defining events in the history of Communist Poland. Walesa's act of defiance launched the strike that began his workers' movement.

Walesa immediately became the de facto leader of the strike. The workers were openly making political as well as economic demands. Walesa was insisting on greater freedom of expression and the right to form trade unions free of Communist Party control. As the strike spread across the Baltic Coast, the prime minister and several high-ranking party officials were dismissed in a party shakeup. Walesa was encouraged by what he saw as a small victory. Because of this, when party leader Gierek promised democratization of the official unions, Walesa held firm. "A change in personnel does not interest me," said Walesa. "What I want is the freedom of the unions, and I don't care who negotiates that."

The strike had spread beyond the Baltic region to involve over 300,000 workers. On August 31, Walesa was summoned to Warsaw and began negotiations with Deputy Prime Minister Mieczyslaw Jagielski. That day the two men signed an accord, known as the Gdansk Agreement, granting workers the right to form independent unions and to strike. The government also pledged to grant wage increases, to relax censorship, to broadcast Roman Catholic Mass on Sundays, and to release jailed members of the Committee for Social Self-Defense. It was an astonishing victory—the first time such rights had ever been conceded in a Soviet bloc country.

The first and only free trade union in the Eastern bloc—Solidarity—was born. Suddenly the Lenin Shipyard, and Walesa himself, became a symbol for dissidents trying to throw off the yoke of totalitarianism throughout Eastern Europe. Walesa knew he'd won the proverbial battle but not yet the war against Communist rule. He denied charges that he was opposed to the Communist system. He described himself as "a union man" simply trying to deal with workers' problems, and he always struck a patriotic note. "Those who brought us to this present situation in our country are antisocialist," he said. "We in the unions are the upholders of socialism."

Walesa was walking a fine line with the authorities. Everyone could see that he was quickly becoming the enfant terrible of the Soviet-controlled East bloc. The one-time unemployed electrician had risen to become an international figure, the embodiment of the dreams of millions of Poles for a better life. At mass rallies Poles followed the song "God Save Poland" with chants of "Long live Walesa" and "May he live 100 years." By jumping over the fence and landing firmly on his feet, he'd won the loyalty of millions of Polish workers. Walesa was opposed to any system that "makes people forget they are human beings." This struck at the heart of the Communist system.

When the strike ended, officials at the regional housing board finally responded to the Walesas' request for a larger apartment, a request that had gone unanswered for years. Apparently the authorities did not want the world to learn how a Polish worker—and now a labor leader—with a good number of children lived. In a single night the authorities vacated a six-room, second-story apartment for the Walesa family to move into.

As chairman of Solidarity, Walesa had a salary that was equivalent to $333 a month, about the same as that of a shipyard worker. At the Gdansk shipyard, many of his fellow workers were eager to talk to Walesa whenever he visited the canteen. Agents would surround them with tape recorders to include their conversations in their political dossiers. Those who were seen with Walesa would later find that they were summoned to the management offices for a "conversation" with the police. Given these circumstances, Walesa decided it would be wiser to hold his press conferences outside the shipyards.

Even leaving the shipyard was no longer a routine matter. On his way home from work one day, Walesa was approached by a man who said he'd been hired to assassinate him. The assassin, however, had a sudden change of heart when he met the charismatic union activist in person. When Walesa wanted to attend Solidarity meetings, he eluded authorities by driving home accompanied by a lookalike. The stocky, mustachioed imposter would emerge from Walesa's minivan and enter Walesa's apartment building. The real Walesa was then whisked away, lying face down in the back of the van.

Walesa's family had to grow accustomed to a steady stream of visitors who disrupted their household. At first they left the doors open for the crowds of journalists and visitors who came and went freely. Family matters and Solidarity matters overlapped. Eventually the disruptions became too much for Walesa to bear. Because he knew that his apartment was bugged, he began to have journalists wait for him in the square in front of St. Brygida's Church in Gdansk, a spiritual home of the Solidarity movement. As a public speaker who was usually pressed for time, he would get furious if, when he arrived at the square, the television crews were still laying cables and preparing for an interview.

Walesa had won the day by establishing Solidarity as the first and only free trade union in the Soviet bloc, but he had not forgotten the massacre of workers at the protests in 1970. Their deaths still angered him so much that one of his obsessions became the building of a monument to honor the more than 100 slain workers. The towering monument of three crosses was unveiled on the tenth anniversary of the December 1970 demonstrations. The dedication was attended by party leaders. From then on it stood as a constant reproach to the authorities. At night, the police would come and take away the flowers that thousands of people placed at the base.

The year 1981 opened with increased worker militancy. Despite the government's agreement with Walesa, officials didn't deliver on their promise to establish a five-day work week by granting free Saturdays. Walesa had no choice but to go along with a boycott of work on Saturday, January 10. In the meantime, he had already scheduled a trip to meet with the pope in Rome. He and his wife Danuta were blessed by John Paul II in an unforgettable meeting at the Vatican in January 1981. It was their first trip abroad, and a dream come true, though one that was marred by a threat on Walesa's life. Walesa learned that the Red Brigades, a terrorist organization based in Italy, was planning to assassinate him. As a result, he and Danuta were surrounded day and night by a team of bodyguards.

Walesa was reelected chairman of Solidarity during the organization's second session of the congress, in the fall of 1981. Always the negotiator, Walesa tried to resist the rise of radical factions within his organization. But the radical factions caught Walesa off guard by calling for a national vote on the continuance of the Communist Party in Poland.

Premier and Communist Party leader General Wojciech Jaruzelski reacted brutally. His forces trashed Solidarity's headquarters, declared the 10-million-strong union illegal, arrested Walesa and other leaders, and declared martial law. Tank battalions rolled into the Gdansk Shipyard, crashing through the gates where Walesa's monument towered. Citizens—including old people and children—were arrested on the streets and beaten indiscriminately. Walesa was arrested and jailed, and overnight his free trade movement was crushed.

Letters from Pope John Paul II supporting Walesa's plea for peaceful talks to restore freedom were sent directly to the new government of General Jaruzelski. The pope inspired in Poles feelings of freedom that they had never known, not only because he was a fellow Pole, but because the people felt that behind him stood God. During the eight days of the pope's second visit to Poland in June of 1982, the crowds unfurled their red and white Solidarity banners and shouted, "Lech Walesa! Lech Walesa!"

Finally, on November 15, 1982, Walesa was freed. He emerged from 11 months of solitary confinement to find his Solidarity union destroyed by martial law. He was put under constant surveillance. Yet, as best he could, he continued to operate Solidarity as an underground movement. Somehow he managed to publish *Solidarity Weekly* with printing presses and radio equipment smuggled in from the West. The government said that Walesa was a has-been, "the former head of a former union." But Walesa was still getting his message—Solidarity Lives!—out to the rest of the world.

The information campaign was so successful that street protests were organized in the United States to show support for Walesa's courageous efforts. The West was demonstrating solidarity with Solidarity. In the fall of 1983 the people of Poland rejoiced when Walesa was awarded the Nobel Peace Prize. Walesa was involved in a very common Polish activity, picking mushrooms with friends in the woods, when Western television crews arrived with the good news. The mushroom-hunting party grabbed the new laureate and tossed him in the air. When he got his breath back, Walesa beamed and told the world: "The world recognizes Solidarity's ideals and struggles."

For Walesa, as well as for most Poles, receiving the Nobel Prize was a vindication of the only free trade union in the Soviet bloc. To the Communist authorities, however, it was a slap in the face. The government was beginning to realize that taking aggressive measures against a Nobel Peace Prize laureate was not wise. In 1986, for example, Walesa

> "The world recognizes Solidarity's ideals and struggles."

was able to openly organize a legal defense committee for Solidarity activists. The following year marked a real turning point. For the first time John Paul II, so beloved by the Poles, was able to travel to the forbidden city of Gdansk, and better yet, to nearby Zaspa, where Walesa was living. Walesa was able to receive communion from John Paul II.

Walesa was aware that the pope could not solve Poland's problems, but he would tell the world about the Poles' desire for a new government. During the pope's third visit to Poland, a million people in Warsaw raised their arms in the air and extended the "V" sign for victory as the pope blessed them. Seeing the hundreds of Solidarity banners, and feeling the enthusiasm of a crowd no longer cowed by the police, Walesa became sure that the era of intimidation would soon be over.

In October of 1987, the Communists called a national referendum on the question of whether the "progressive economic and social reforms" taking place in Poland should continue. Walesa made it clear that the nation should refuse to go along with what was seen as an obvious propaganda ploy. In reality, the government's economic plans consisted merely of halfhearted alternatives to the status quo and one or two pieties about improving the quality of life. Walesa's response to the government's double-talk was concrete. He called for a boycott of the elections. He knew that Poland needed a market economy and freely elected representatives.

Despite the government's claims that Walesa was merely a private citizen, he had become an institution, a fact taken for granted as much by the party leaders as by ordinary Poles. Walesa went on granting interviews, speaking until he was hoarse, and quietly plotting ways to combat communism. He had become very adept at handling the press.

In his talks with journalists Walesa frequently used analogies. When asked under what conditions he would hold talks with the government, he compared the situation in Poland to a chessboard on which the government wanted to be queen—and use Solidarity as one of its pawns. Concerning *perestroika*, the economic restructuring now openly debated in the Soviet Union, Walesa would say only that one privately owned café in Moscow did not constitute economic reform.

Walesa was enthusiastic about the new *perestroika* advocated by Soviet premier Mikhail Gorbachev and had growing hopes that it would spread to Poland. What pained him most was the visible increase of poverty in Poland. When in the spring of 1988 the press announced that Gorbachev would visit, many greeted the news with cynicism. But Walesa was convinced that the visit could be another turning point for Poland.

Walesa followed Gorbachev's visit closely. When Gorbachev appeared on television, Walesa was heartened to hear the Soviet leader declare an era of new relations between the two states. Walesa was eager to learn what this new era meant, but at that point a government spokesman appeared on his television screen. The news announcer said that, according to the government spokesman, Solidarity would remain a thing of the past. The ban on the free trade movement would not be lifted. "We'll just see about that," said Walesa, switching off the television set.

Three weeks later, in April, miners in Silesia began a series of strikes. The Silesian miners' strike encouraged Walesa greatly, especially because in earlier demonstrations the miners had usually been the last to get involved. This time, however, the miners went so far as to demand the establishment of free trade unions.

Walesa demanded that the government begin negotiations. Meanwhile, over the next few days, the number of mines on strike rose from 6 to 16. All of them demanded one thing above all else: the legalization of Solidarity. Walesa had not encouraged or authorized the strikes, but he did not discourage them either. The 1988 miners' strikes managed

Solidarity leader and presidential candidate Lech Walesa going home just after voting in Gdansk for the second round of the presidential election. (AP/Wide World Photos)

to rejuvenate the optimism that had fueled the 1980 strike. Walesa, as head of the still-banned Solidarity, was now 44 years old. To many he seemed tired and less passionate than the Walesa they remembered from eight years before.

Nevertheless, on behalf of the strikers, Walesa on August 31 finally met, virtually as an equal, with the heads of government. Solidarity set one condition—that it be made legal again. The authorities, however, held firm in their position. Solidarity would not be officially recognized—at least not until after further negotiations. For Walesa, it was a disappointing loss. He felt he had been duped into negotiations that produced little progress. After nine days he told the workers that the end of their strike marked a "truce, not a defeat."

Things seemed as bad as ever at the beginning of 1989, but it proved to be a year of surprises for Poland and all of Eastern Europe. The Soviet Union, under Gorbachev, eased its grip on its satellites in Eastern Europe, and the first real changes appeared in Poland. Gorbachev now warned the Polish Communist government that it could not govern without the support of Solidarity. Gorbachev pressured Jaruzelski to enlist the help of Solidarity.

Finally, the troubled Jaruzelski seemed to have nowhere to turn. Only his foe, Lech Walesa, could salvage the Polish economy by breaking the political deadlock. In 1989 Jaruzelski asked Walesa for advice. The invitation was as welcome as it was unexpected. After meeting with Walesa, Jaruzelski legalized Solidarity and invited the union to join him in a coalition government. Walesa's dream was fulfilled: Solidarity would emerge as a genuine political party. Walesa expressed hope that the talks would "become the beginning of the road for democracy and a free Poland."

In accords signed between Solidarity and the government, free elections to the newly restored 100-seat parliament, called the National Assembly, were set for June of 1989. A constitution was drafted, and Poland was well on its way to becoming the first Communist state to evolve into a democracy. In the June elections, Solidarity was swept to victory. In a stunning rebuke to the Communist Party, Polish voters gave Solidarity candidates a huge victory in Poland's first competitive elections in four decades.

Of the 100 Senate seats, 96 went to Solidarity candidates. Most of the 460 seats in the lower house, or Assembly, were allocated exclusively to the Communist Party as part of the pre-election agreement, and its candidates ran unopposed. Jaruzelski, therefore, was elected president because the new parliament had reserved a large block of seats for Communists. Even so, Jaruzelski told other party leaders that the voters had handed them a stunning defeat. "Our defeat is total," Jaruzelski said.

The only question left to decide was who would lead the new government as prime minister. Most Poles expected Walesa to head the coalition government, but he held back for several reasons. He felt it would be wiser to wait until the new government—still largely controlled by Communists—faltered. Instead, one of Walesa's closest advisers, Tadeusz Mazowiecki, was chosen by Walesa and Jaruzelski as prime minister. He was the first non-Communist prime minister in Eastern Europe in 40 years. "It is an incredible success for our struggle," Walesa told the Polish people. "But let us see it in practice."

The state-run economy was replaced by a free-market system, but as Walesa had predicted, the economy ran into serious trouble. Meanwhile, in April 1990, Walesa was reelected to the post of union president at Solidarity's first official national congress since 1981. Soon he began to criticize Mazowiecki for moving too slowly on economic reform.

Events accelerated when Jaruzelski announced his resignation in September of 1990. The National Assembly voted to hold a nationwide presidential election. All at once the campaign was on—the first campaign for a president to be elected by a vote of the people in Poland's history. Walesa and Mazowiecki led the field of candidates in a bitter campaign that seemed to pit workers against intellectuals.

When the results were in on November 25, 1990, Walesa had won the largest share of the votes but had failed to get a majority. He would now face a dark horse candidate, Stanislaw Tyminski, in a runoff election on December 9. In the end the Poles chose Walesa as their first freely elected president. Most had credited him with making the elections possible in the first place, and Walesa vowed not to disappoint them. "This is a victory not for me but for all of Poland," he declared. "I will serve you all."

Saturday, December 22, 1990, was a historic day in Poland. Before a packed crowd in the National Assembly, Walesa was sworn in as president. In becoming president, however, Walesa embarked on a course that was in many ways bolder than the one he started in 1980. With his election to the presidency, Poland became a model for other Eastern European countries that were changing from communism to democratic forms of government.

Unfortunately, great revolutionaries do not always make great leaders. Somehow Walesa had lost the mass adulation he had enjoyed in 1980, when Solidarity alone stood up to Poland's Communist regime. After he took office, polls showed broad dissatisfaction with Walesa's performance. Many argued that he was simply unqualified to run a government—nor did his confrontational style help him deal with parliamentary squabbles and scandals.

> "This is a victory not for me but for all of Poland. I will serve you all."

In 1993, following a no-confidence vote in parliament, he dissolved the body and called elections. But instead of working to unite reform forces, he set about turning one against the other in an apparent attempt to increase his power. The ploy only helped the leftist parties—those urging faster reform—and they gained a majority in Parliament.

While Walesa will always be hailed abroad as a great revolutionary, in Poland he has become the butt of endless political jokes because of his personality, which has been described as divisive, hectoring, and unstatesmanlike. His fall from grace reflects the profound ambivalence many Poles feel about the revolution sparked by Walesa. After years of austerity, unemployment is growing, and privatization of inefficient state-run enterprises is proving harder to implement than anyone expected.

Walesa is a leader who receives little credit for the benefits brought by his revolution. In fact, he was defeated by a Communist Party candidate in the 1996 elections. Out of work, ironically, Walesa has returned to his old job—as a shipyard electrician. He complains bitterly that he has gotten a large share of the blame for the downside—lost jobs and inflation—and little credit for his accomplishments. "In 50 years there will be monuments for me all over this country and people will lay wreaths every chance they get," Walesa has said. "Then I'll kick my coffin and shout, 'Where were you when I needed you?'"

Whatever his shortcomings, he cannot easily be written off in the future. Lech Walesa will forever be remembered as the man who lit a spark that spread like wildfire across Eastern Europe, leading to the disintegration of the Communist bloc.

Perhaps his vision is summed up best in the final words of his autobiography. "There will come a time, which I won't live to see, when narrow Polish problems have been brushed aside, replaced by harmony and peace over our entire planet. Until that time we have work to do."

Whatever the future of Poland, says Dennis Vnenchak in his book *Lech Walesa and Poland*, Walesa's achievements will always overshadow his shortcomings. "The electrician from Gdansk achieved for Poland real political independence from the Soviet Union," Vnenchak wrote. "Forty-five years of Soviet-sponsored communist rule had come to an end. Poland's freedom had been won, in large measure because of the efforts of an electrician from the Lenin Shipyards at Gdansk. More than any other Pole, Lech Walesa had made that happen."

Chronology

September 29, 1943	Born in Popowo, Poland
May 1945	Father dies
1959	Starts a three-year course at the trade school in Lipno
1965	Conscripted into the Polish army for two years' military service
1967	Moves to Baltic seaport of Gdansk and becomes an electrician
November 8, 1969	Marries Danuta Golos
February 1976	Loses his job at the shipyard after speaking out against the Polish authorities
April 29, 1978	The Baltic Committee for Free and Independent Trade Unions is set up by Lech Walesa and other dissident workers
December 16, 1979	Seven thousand people gather at the shipyard in Gdansk to remember those killed in 1970. Walesa calls on them to set up independent groups to protect themselves
August 31, 1980	The Gdansk Agreement is signed. Independent trade unions are now legal
November 1980	Solidarity is registered as an independent trade union, the first in a Soviet-controlled country

December 12, 1981	Solidarity leaders are rounded up. Martial law is declared. Walesa begins an 11-month internment
April 1983	Returns to work at Lenin Shipyard
December 1983	Awarded the Nobel Peace Prize
April 17, 1989	Solidarity is legalized
June 1989	Solidarity wins 96 out of 100 Senate seats. Allowed to run for only 161 of the 360 seats in the lower house, Solidarity wins all 161.
July 1989	General Jaruzelski is elected president and asks Solidarity to form a coalition government with the party
August 24, 1989	Poland's parliament elects the Eastern bloc's first non-Communist prime minister in over 40 years
December 22, 1990	Walesa is sworn in as president

Further Reading

Angel, Ann, and Mary Craig. *Lech Walesa: Champion of Freedom for Poland*. Milwaukee: G. Stevens Children's Books, 1992. Presents events in the life of the Polish union leader in the context of his nonviolent struggle.

Laso, Caroline. *Lech Walesa and Poland*. New York: Franklin Watts, 1994. Examines Poland's history, with particular emphasis on the role of Walesa.

Stefoff, Rebecca. *Lech Walesa: The Road to Democracy*. New York: Fawcett Columbine, 1992. Traces the life of the Polish union organizer, including his role in gaining recognition for Solidarity, his winning the Nobel Prize, and his election as Poland's first democratic president.

Father Jerzy Popieluszko was the spiritual leader of the Solidarity movement. (Church of the American Conception)

Father Jerzy Popieluszko

When the body of Father Jerzy Popieluszko—regarded as the spiritual leader of the outlawed Solidarity trade union in Poland—was fished from a reservoir in the fall of 1984, all of Poland mourned the death of this charismatic young clergyman. The following spring, when the entire Polish nation saw four members of the secret police openly tried and convicted for the murder of Popieluszko, it was a unique event for a Soviet bloc country.

Few people, inside or outside Poland, believed that the trial revealed the whole truth about Father Jerzy's death. But the spectacle of a secret-police officer being called to account for crimes against a dissident priest was one of the first cracks in a Communist system that would crumble five years later. What mattered most was that the trial had happened at all, and that the Polish people learned about it from television, the newspapers, and half-hour radio broadcasts every night.

Father Jerzy had become a symbol of uncompromising faith for the Polish people. His death created a martyr for Solidarity, the first free trade union in a Soviet bloc country. His words, spoken in his weekly Mass for the Country, haunted the Communist dictatorship and helped inspire a whole generation of Polish workers to throw off the yoke of their Soviet overlords. "If we must die," said Father Jerzy, always aware that his life was in

> jeopardy, "then it is better to meet death while defending a worthwhile cause than sitting back and letting an injustice take place."

Jerzy was born on September 14, 1947, into the peasant family of Marianna and Wladyslaw Popieluszko in the small Polish village of Okopy. Only two days after his birth, he was baptized and given the name Alfonse after his godfather, a name he used throughout his childhood. Only later, when he entered the Warsaw Seminary, was he persuaded to change his name to Jerzy. Alfonse, he was reminded, was the name of anyone of questionable repute in Polish folk songs. It was not a suitable name for a priest.

By Polish standards, Jerzy's parents were neither rich nor poor. They owned a few acres of land and some cows. In winter the whole family slept together in his parents' bedroom, the only room that was heated, by a huge stove. His parents worked hard to raise their four children. When Jerzy was born with yellowish ulcers covering his body, the doctor said it was the result of his mother working too hard during pregnancy.

> "If we must die, then it is better to meet death while defending a worthwhile cause than sitting back and letting an injustice take place."

Jerzy was a good child, always smiling and content. He never complained, and he endured suffering stoically. Jerzy's life, like that of other peasant boys, was not easy. He was expected to put in his share of work at home and in the fields, after school and during his holidays. His parents had little time to share affection with their four children, but Jerzy grew up with a deep respect for his parents and loved them dearly. Jerzy's family was Roman Catholic, as were most people in the region. The Church was an important and central facet of his family life.

Though his parish church, like his school, was some five miles away, every morning at seven o'clock Jerzy was there for Mass, serving as an altar boy. He never saw the long early morning trek as a sacrifice. To him it was the normal duty of a Catholic boy who naturally took his faith very seriously.

Jerzy finished the seventh grade of his primary school and entered the local secondary school in 1961. His new school had been built for peasant boys after World War II by a young and dedicated priest. Though it received no state support, the school's academic standards were equal to those of the best schools in the country. While most other Polish schools were secular, teaching the atheistic philosophy of Marxism-Leninism, Jerzy was educated by practicing Catholics who nurtured his religious convictions.

He was an average student who excelled in history and literature but never in the sciences. A former teacher remembers him as an inquisitive boy and "a modest, truthful child, always ready to help others." A bit of a loner, he used to leave home an hour early and walk to church by himself. As he explained to his friends, there were so many things for him to think about. They nicknamed him "philosopher" for his tendency to weigh all of life's problems from a moral standpoint.

Jerzy had been drawn to the priesthood all his life, so it was no surprise when he decided to enter the Warsaw Seminary of John the Baptist. According to Jerzy's mother, he chose the Warsaw Seminary because of its proximity to the Place of the Immaculate One, a Franciscan friary. The friary had been built by his hero, Father Kolbe, a Polish saint who sacrificed his own life for another prisoner in a concentration camp. All his life Father Jerzy was captivated by stories about the Polish saint.

On June 24, 1965, Jerzy entered the seminary to begin the seven years of preparation for the priesthood. That year, however, the Polish Church was celebrating its first millennium and the officially atheistic government was cracking down on the Church. After only a year in the seminary Jerzy was transferred to the military. Conscription into the army was a convenient method the government used to break the spirits of seminarians.

For the next two years he served in three special clerical units in Poland, a Communist country that nevertheless allowed church services so that the state would not have to compete with Roman Catholic theology. Often in Jerzy's life the underlying tension between church and state rose to the surface. One day a Communist army officer discovered a set of rosary beads in Jerzy's hand and gruffly ordered him to trample on it. "If you will not tread on the rosary then I will tread on you," he was told. Jerzy refused. For this he was badly beaten and tossed into a jail cell for 30 days. This test of courage was Jerzy's first taste of the difficulties he would be facing as a Catholic priest. Ironically, this experience, which was supposed to break him psychologically, backfired by teaching Jerzy how to overcome fear.

When he returned to Warsaw in 1968 Father Jerzy had to undergo a serious operation on his thyroid gland. After that his bouts of illness never ended. But finally, on May 28, 1972, Jerzy was ordained a priest by Cardinal Stefan Wyszynski, Primate of Poland. His first post was in the parish of Zabkie, just outside Warsaw. All the parishioners still remember Father Jerzy as a man with a saintly sense of duty. He helped anyone who was in need, working far beyond the limits of his frail health.

Father Jerzy was now the busy young assistant in an active parish. He led Mass, heard confession, visited the sick and troubled, conducted funerals, and held catechism classes for children and teenagers. Most of his free time was spent in a nearby hospital ministering to the infirm. Jerzy even started a rosary circle for young people, a prayer group where he taught the meaning of practicing Christianity in everyday life.

In October 1975, after three years in Zabkie, Father Jerzy was transferred to the parish of The Mother of God, Queen of Poland, in another Warsaw suburb called Anin. He spent three years there, and in May 1978 was promoted to pastor and moved to the Parish of the Infant Jesus in Zoliborz, a workers' district of Warsaw. He threw himself into his work and was an instant hit with all the children and young people. But failing health and a heavy workload were beginning to wear him down. While saying Mass one day, he collapsed, unconscious, at the altar. For the first time, another priest had to finish a service Father Jerzy had begun.

After only one year at the Infant Jesus parish, the exhausted priest was moved to the academic church of St. Anna in order to lighten his workload. There he was put in charge of the medical school students, organizing lectures, discussions, retreats, and summer camps. Father Jerzy was so popular with the students that when he left St. Anna's for a new church, St. Stanislaw Kostka, in May 1980, his students simply followed him.

When Father Jerzy was appointed resident priest at the church of St. Stanislaw Kostka, a position usually reserved for retired priests, he was only 32 years old, but his medical condition required a quiet life free from strain. The new resident priest at St. Stanislaw never let his health slow him down. By then he had a small army—not just medical students, but doctors and nurses, who helped him organize the health services for Pope John Paul II's first visit to Poland in the summer of 1979, and again four years later. Far from fading into retirement, Father Jerzy would soon embark on what was to become the most energetic part of his life.

In the summer of 1980, a peaceful national revolution led by the Solidarity movement was beginning, led by Lech Walesa, an ordinary shipyard worker in Gdansk. All the opposition groups, despite differences in their political programs, followed the example of peaceful dissent the Church had been preaching for years. Like most Polish priests and bishops, Father Jerzy had a Christian vision of humanity that advocated resistance to repression through moral revival.

In August 1980 almost all of Poland's industrial plants staged strikes in support of the Gdansk shipyard. A sympathy strike was being organized in the Warsaw steel plant, and workers from the plant asked the diocese to find a priest to help them. At St. Stanislaw Kostka, the priest who was handling the matter ran into Father Jerzy. He explained the situation to him, and he immediately agreed to help. He would celebrate Mass for them at once.

When Father Jerzy first entered the gates of the plant, crowds of workers began smiling, crying, and clapping. He was astonished. "At first I thought that there was someone important right behind me," Father Jerzy said. "But they were clapping at me—the first priest in the history of this plant to enter at the main gate. It then crossed my mind that this applause was for the Church, which for the last 30 years had constantly knocked at the gates of the industrial plants."

"Thanks be to God!" was roared by thousands of workers at the first Mass Father Jerzy celebrated with the workers that day. The experience left a deep impression on him, and an ironclad bond was forged between him and the striking steelworkers.

> "At first I thought that there was someone important right behind me. But they were clapping at me—the first priest in the history of this plant to enter at the main gate. It then crossed my mind that this applause was for the Church, which for the last 30 years had constantly knocked at the gates of the industrial plants."

Day and night he remained with them, celebrating Mass, hearing confessions, and lifting their spirits. When the strike ended, he accepted a job as plant chaplain. Father Jerzy's St. Stanislaw Kostka's became the official "parish" church for the Warsaw steel works.

A few months later, on December 13, 1981, after workers called for a national referendum on the continuance of the Communist Party in Poland, the government decided it had had enough. Martial law was declared in Poland. Lech Walesa and other Solidarity leaders were arrested and put on trial. Father Jerzy kept in close contact with the workers, meanwhile. He believed that this was his duty as a priest. He was the only priest in regular attendance at the trials, usually sitting in the front row with the families of prosecuted workers. The presence of a priest in the courtroom was undoubtedly an embarrassment to the authorities.

Father Jerzy knew how much it meant to the jailed Solidarity activists to see that their families were being looked after properly. He was always there to provide emotional comfort and material help, especially for families with children whose fathers had been fired from their jobs. After martial law was declared he set up the first charitable center for worker families at St. Stanislaw Kostka. He could always recite from memory a long list of people and the exact items they needed: shoes for this one, an overcoat for another, milk for someone's baby, foreign medicines for someone else.

It was at the trials of the Warsaw steelworkers that Father Jerzy first thought about holding special Masses for imprisoned workers. In January 1982, just one month after the introduction of martial law, anyone making "anti-state pronouncements" was threatened with the death penalty. But Father Jerzy would not be silenced. He delivered his first "patriotic sermon" in what became known as his monthly Masses for the Country. It consisted of one single sentence: "Because freedom of speech has been taken away from us by the introduction of martial law, let us, while listening to the voice of our heart and conscience, think of those brothers and sisters who have been deprived of their freedom." Three minutes of silence followed.

Father Jerzy's seven o'clock Mass on the last Sunday evening of each month became a regular feature at St. Stanislaw Kostka. The Mass drew larger and larger crowds of people from all walks of life.

Father Jerzy spoke of "the many crimes of Cain" and of "a nation terrorized by military forces" and of "people detained and brought to trial, their only guilt being their determination to remain faithful to the ideals of Solidarity." He described "attempts to send healthy internees to mental institutions" and "the beating and ill-treatment of the many prisoners in the internment camps scattered throughout Poland." He pointed out that "Christ was killed on the Cross by His own countrymen, in His own country. Today our brothers are also being killed by their fellow countrymen." While condemning evil, he also spoke out against any thought of hatred or revenge.

Father Jerzy's vision had little appeal for the Polish atheist authorities. While thousands of people celebrated Mass, a cordon of riot squad police stood just a few yards away armed with a water cannon. So as not to provoke the military, Father Jerzy reminded his followers that this was a church service, not a political rally, and asked that no flags or banners be displayed inside or outside the church.

At first the authorities tried to silence Father Jerzy by pressuring the

"Because freedom of speech has been taken away from us by the introduction of martial law, let us, while listening to the voice of our heart and conscience, think of those brothers and sisters who have been deprived of their freedom."

Church to curb his critical statements. When that failed, they tried a different tactic: they pressured Father Jerzy directly. The presbytery of the church was vandalized by "unknown hooligans." On the night of December 13, 1982, when Father Jerzy had just finished preparing Christmas gifts for the children in a nearby hospital, a bomb was thrown into his apartment. The bomb, with a detonator inside it, was attached to a brick. Although it did not explode, it was clear that the perpetrators had tried to kill him.

Day and night Father Jerzy was followed by the state secret police. He tried to ignore them and joked that the only "tail" whose company he enjoyed was that of his little black mongrel dog. The pet had been a present to Father Jerzy in 1983 and was given the English name "Tiney" on account of his small size. "Tiney" pronounced by a Pole sounds very like "Tajniak"—the derogatory term for a secret policeman. And as Tiney followed Father Jerzy everywhere, he soon became "Tajniak."

Father Jerzy was also convinced that his telephone was bugged. Again, he made light of it. Whenever a call was interrupted by odd noises on the line, he'd tell the caller that "a crow is probably sitting on the line again." Crow—*wrona* in Polish—was another pun. WRON, the "Military Council of National Salvation," was an acronym widely used to describe the Communist regime.

The vicious campaign against Father Jerzy escalated dramatically, especially after the May 1983 Mass for the Country. In July of 1983, an official investigation was ordered into Father Jerzy's alleged "abuse of freedom of conscience and religion." He was said to have continually included "political slanders against the state authorities" in his sermons.

Conveniently, when the Ministry of Religious Affairs searched his apartment, they "found" thousands of underground leaflets known as samizdat, in addition to 38 pieces of ammunition and some explosives, including hand grenades.

It was clear that the "evidence" had been planted. Nevertheless, Father Jerzy was arrested and forced to spend one night in a jail cell. He was released the next day following the intervention of the Polish Episcopate, the Polish arm of the Roman Catholic Church.

All charges against him were suspended under the amnesty that marked the 40th anniversary of Communist Poland. It was clear that news of the amnesty brought great relief to Father Jerzy. But he knew all too well that it was just a temporary reprieve. Under the terms of the amnesty, he had to refrain from similar "political actions" for two and a half years. That would mean the end of the Masses for the Country, and Father Jerzy would not allow that to happen.

During this time, Father Jerzy was also becoming very unpopular in Moscow. In September 1983, the Soviet newspaper *Izvestia* wrote that "he has turned his apartment into a warehouse of literature, and he closely cooperates with inveterate counterrevolutionaries." Although this negative publicity was making life difficult for Father Jerzy, he was bolstered by the approval of the highest Roman Catholic authorities. In recognition of his pastoral work, the Polish pope, John Paul II, sent him a rosary through Bishop Kraszewski in February 1984. "Please tell him that I am with him, with all my heart," the pope said. Father Jerzy considered the gift his greatest treasure. For a time, he believed that nothing bad could really happen to him with such a protector in the Vatican.

But soon it became clear that Father Jerzy had an inkling of what was in store for him. He began to smoke incessantly. To calm his nerves, he began to spend his free time tending the garden on the parish grounds. When he visited his parents two weeks before his death, he stayed longer than usual. Before leaving he walked around the whole house and the farm as if he wanted to say goodbye to all the memories of his childhood. When a friend visited him in September, he

Father Jerzy speaking to his congregation, just before he was kidnapped. (AP/Wide World Photos)

found Father Jerzy engrossed in writing. "I am making my will," he informed the visitor. After his murder, a will was never found.

In the fall, the Ministry of the Interior called for "decisive and speedy action" against antistate priests and named Father Jerzy as the first priest who had to be dealt with. What this meant was anyone's guess. One day in mid-October, three men tailed the priest as he set out in his car. They pulled up beside him, passed his car, and pushed Father Jerzy and his driver off the road. One man, powerfully built and wearing a ski mask, heaved a brick at the priest's window, hoping to cause an accident, but he missed.

A week later, on Friday October 19, Father Jerzy was expected in Bydgoszcz, a town in northern Poland, some 300 miles from Warsaw. At about 9:30 a.m. he left for Bydgoszcz in a car driven by his friend Waldemar Chrostowski. Outside Warsaw, however, they were stopped by the traffic police. After a short conversation with the police, they were allowed to continue the journey. At 6 o'clock in the evening, Father Jerzy began the celebration of what was to be his last Mass. His three murderers were already waiting for him in a car just outside the presbytery.

Soon after they left church that evening by car, Father Jerzy and his driver noticed that they were being followed. Suddenly, a Fiat caught up with them and overtook Father Jerzy and his driver. Father Jerzy's car pulled to the side of the road, and then he was dragged out of his car into the back of the Fiat, where policemen used their fists and a wooden club to beat him into unconsciousness. Then, although he was unconscious, he was handcuffed and gagged and flung into the trunk. Father Jerzy had been kidnapped.

His driver, Chrostowski, was ordered into the front of the Fiat, but managed to leap from the speeding car and went to seek help. Meanwhile, the kidnappers continued to drive until Father Jerzy regained consciousness. Father Jerzy began shouting loudly and banging against the lid of the trunk. When they stopped the Fiat at the side of the road and opened the trunk, Father Jerzy tried to escape. By the time they had gotten out of the car, Father Jerzy was already running away, shouting for help. "Save me! Save me! Please spare my life!"

The three abductors caught him again and beat him senseless with a wooden club. The men gagged him and tied him down more thoroughly in the trunk of the Fiat. The exhausted clergyman managed to survive this latest beating and regained consciousness. When he tried to force open the lid of the trunk a second time, he was pummeled again.

His mouth was sealed with masking tape, which severely obstructed his breathing, according to testimony in the subsequent trial of his captors. Having been beaten several times now, the priest was already in shock when he was dragged to a dam on a local reservoir and flung into the water. Weighted down by a bag of stones fastened to his feet, his body sank. No one will never know for certain whether he was still alive when his body was tossed into the water.

When Father Jerzy's driver, Chrostowski, sounded the alarm about the priest's kidnapping, Polish emotions exploded. The murder couldn't be covered up. The following day, people flocked to St. Stanislaw Kostka Church to join in prayers. Various groups and individuals, both in Poland and abroad, voiced their shock and horror at this outrageous crime. On October 21, Lech Walesa came to Father Jerzy's church and publicly warned the perpetrators of this vicious crime: "If a hair on Father Popieluszko's head has been harmed, then someone will be taking upon himself a terrible responsibility."

The following day 15 intellectuals sent a letter to General Wojciech Jaruzelski, placing the blame for the abduction on government authorities. Two days later, during his weekly Wednesday audience at the Vatican, John Paul II expressed his "solidarity with Warsaw's clergy and parishioners in the face of this anti-human act of open violence against a priest." The Pope asked the whole Church to pray for Father Jerzy, and appealed to the consciences of those guilty of the crime to release Father Jerzy if he were still alive.

Great bitterness was aroused in the Polish people by numerous cases of police provocation and intimidation of Father Jerzy's friends. Workers who organized prayer meetings for Father Jerzy in the Warsaw steel plant were interrogated by the secret police. And on October 22 several men tried to "instigate disorder" in front of the church of St. Stanislaw Kostka, according to the government. The following day a similar incident occurred. This time there were more drunken men. Not far away the militia was waiting, ready to move in "to restore law and order." The same afternoon an explosive device went off just outside the presbytery.

In this atmosphere of uncertainty and speculation, the identity of the kidnappers was finally released. On October 29, 10 days after Father Jerzy's death, the ministry announced that the body of Father Jerzy had been found in the waters of the Wloclawek reservoir. The parishioners at St. Stanislaw Kostka Church fell to their knees in loud cries when they heard the announcement at Mass that night. By midnight, thousands of candles and lamps had been lit and placed alongside the metal fence surrounding the church grounds. The fence itself was barely visible, having been covered in flowers.

A few days later, Father Jerzy was laid to rest on the grounds of St. Stanislaw's. His parents picked Warsaw, and especially the church where he worked and where he was loved so much, as the suitable place for his burial. All week long mourners gathered outside St. Stanislaw's. Tens of thousands of people gathered in the square in front of the chapel, and the side streets were packed waiting for his funeral service. It was bitterly cold, but the vigil continued through the night. The front of the main altar overflowed with flowers. A bed of candles illuminated the sidewalk around the church as parishioners tacked poems of homage to announcement boards.

Midnight arrived and again Mass was celebrated. At his funeral service the next day, November 2, extracts from Father Jerzy's sermons were read over the loudspeakers. The people listened, repeating in unison after each reading "Overcome evil with good." An ocean of people stretched beyond the gates of the church. The mourners were so tightly wedged that it was difficult for those crying to wipe away their tears.

At the end of the Mass the farewell speeches began. The most moving was a short speech by Karol Szadurski, who represented the Warsaw steel plant. He called out: "Father Jerzy, can you hear the tolling bells of freedom? Can you hear our hearts praying? The Pope, the Primate and your parish priest are praying with us. Listen with us and above us. Your ark, the Solidarity of hearts, drifts along, carrying more and more of us with it."

The new martyr of the Solidarity movement was buried on the grounds of the church that he had made into a symbol of opposition to Communist rule. The slain priest's grave site there in his old church in the suburbs of Warsaw gave Solidarity militants a rallying point for future protests. As a quarter of a million Poles paid their last respects, Father Jerzy was becoming as formidable an opponent in death as he had been in life.

Solidarity activists called for a one-hour strike during his funeral and set up committees in five cities to mourn human rights abuses. Speaking on behalf of all Poles, Lech Walesa, the leader of the banned Solidarity trade union, made a promise to Father Jerzy at his funeral "not to wilt in the face of violence, to respond to lies with the truth and to build a civilization of love."

In the end, Father Jerzy's message of forgiveness did not silence the basic questions being asked by the people: Who were the murderers and on whose orders did they act? From the beginning, the authorities wavered between maintaining that the murder was a "political provocation" against the Polish government perpetrated by government "hard-liners" and the implausible assertion that it was the isolated work of one Communist police captain.

Moreover, the timing of Father Jerzy's death was awkward for the Polish government. It came just as the West had put the crushing of Solidarity behind it and was trying to restore a semblance of normal relations with Poland. But President Ronald Reagan of the United States issued a statement calling Father Jerzy "a champion of Christian values and a courageous spokesman for the cause of liberty."

When the trial for the murder of Father Jerzy opened in October of 1985, the spectacle of a secret police officer being called to account for crimes against a dissident priest made for riveting drama. As the court case unfolded, questions remained about just how far the government of General Wojiech Jaruzelski was prepared to go to implicate high officials of his regime. In holding the trial at all, and allowing the press to cover it, the regime hoped to persuade the world that it had nothing to hide.

During the trial, conducted by the rules of Poland's one-sided judicial system, the court went to great lengths to prove that the affair was definitely not connected to the Ministry of the Interior or other Polish authorities. One of the state prosecutors even hinted that Western circles, bent on destabilizing the Polish regime, were behind the kidnapping. At this point, relative common sense prevailed and that accusation was not pursued. But so one-sided and farcical was the trial that it seemed to be turning into a posthumous examination of the "crimes" of Father Jerzy.

Press coverage of the proceedings was unprecedented in Poland. Warsaw Radio issued hourly bulletins, quoting liberally from the testimony but omitting any evidence that might point to a wider conspiracy. While the nation watched and waited for the outcome of the trial, a movement was growing to propose Father Jerzy for beatification, the first step toward sainthood in the Roman Catholic Church.

More than 20,000 Poles filled the streets outside St. Stanislaw Kostka Church in Warsaw the following January for the monthly Mass for the Country, a tradition begun by Father Jerzy and continued after his death. In the churchyard was a grisly reminder of the crime: a nativity scene in which the Christ child was sheltered inside the open trunk of the same model of car in which Popieluszko was kidnapped and driven to his death.

Meanwhile the story of Father Jerzy's death came out in the courtroom. Police Captain Grzegorz Piotrowski, with no expression of remorse, confessed to beating the priest to death and received a 25-year prison sentence instead of the death penalty the prosecution had requested. When the Polish people heard the sentences, a bitter joke was born and began to circulate in Poland: "Question: Why did Piotrowski get 25 years' imprisonment? Answer: One year for killing Father Jerzy and 24 for messing it up."

The trial did not produce any surprises or implicate any high-level officials. But by exposing the secret police as violent and corrupt, it confirmed what the underground press had been saying for years. Although it was possible that the three men who carried out the murder had acted on their own, even government officials talked of conspiracy in high places. On November 2, a general was suspended and two colonels arrested in connection with the murder.

The killing of a Catholic priest—one who had courageously and uncompromisingly followed his vocation and preached nothing but love and forgiveness—was probably the greatest shock to the Polish people in their postwar history. Silencing Father Jerzy only served to strengthen antigovernment sentiment at home and abroad. And the spirit of the martyred priest would haunt Poland long after the trial came to a close. People from all over Poland came to pray at Father Jerzy's grave and to participate in the Mass that was said for him in his church every evening at seven o'clock.

Finally, an issue of the leading underground newspaper provided a clue as to what the impact of the priest's murder on Solidarity would be: "Father Jerzy Popieluszko is a Solidarity martyr in the most profound sense—by his death he has made it into a truly sacred cause." The killing had given an entirely new complexion to the dissident group. Walesa said the killers wanted to eliminate "not only a man, not only a Pole, not only a priest" but also "the hope that it is possible to avoid violence" in Poland's political life.

Tragically, the death of Father Jerzy seemed to have one good result. It exacted a steep price from the government, because it made the Polish people realize, more than ever before, that the only way to win freedom was through a spiritual revolution. This revolution, begun in August 1980, four years before Father Jerzy's death, succeeded six years after his death when, in December of 1990, Lech Walesa was sworn in as president. Poland was free—and Father Jerzy, though not around to see its freedom, had played a decisive role in obtaining it.

After Father Jerzy's murder, the following extract from his sermons became the one most widely quoted by the Polish people:

> Let us put the truth, like a light, on a candlestick, let us make life in truth shine out, if we do not want our conscience to putrefy. Let us not sell our ideals for a mess of pottage. Let us not sell our ideals by selling our

brothers. It depends on our concern for our innocently imprisoned brothers, on our life in truth, how soon that time comes when we shall share our daily bread again in solidarity and love. At this time, when we need so much strength to regain and uphold our freedom, let us pray to God to fill us with the power of His Spirit, to reawaken the spirit of true solidarity in our hearts.

Father Jerzy's words sustained the Polish people as they continued their struggle to overthrow the Communist government after his death. His teaching and the testament of his life remained with the Polish people long after he died. According to one of his biographers, fellow Pole Grazyna Sikorska, "The death of Father Jerzy made the people of Poland realize, more than ever before, that the only way to acquire freedom is through a spiritual revolution." Father Jerzy's central message, she says, was not lost on the fervently religious Polish people. That message, Sikorska says, was that freedom requires "a renewal of every individual so that an inner interdependence of mind and spirit is acquired and manifests itself outwardly."

To the Polish people, Father Jerzy will always be the embodiment of freedom.

Chronology

September 14, 1947	Born in the Polish village of Okopy
September 1961	Enters a local secondary school
June 24, 1965	Enters the seminary to prepare for priesthood
June, 1966	His education at the seminary interrupted when he is conscripted into the military for two years

May 28, 1972	Ordained a Roman Catholic priest and takes first post in parish of Zabkie, just outside Warsaw
October 1975	Transferred to the parish of The Mother of God, Queen of Poland, in Anin, another Warsaw suburb
May 1978	Promoted to pastor and moves to the Parish of the Infant Jesus in Zoliborz, a workers' district of the city
May 1979	Exhausted and in failing health, he is transferred to the academic church of St. Anna
May 1980	Leaves St. Anna's for a new church, St. Stanislaw Kostka, just outside Warsaw
August 1980	Conducts Mass at Warsaw steel plant as nationwide industrial strikes are staged in support of the Gdansk shipyard
December 13, 1981	Martial law is declared in Poland
January 1982	Attends trials of the Warsaw steelworkers and begins his monthly Masses for the Country
December 13, 1982	A bomb thrown into his apartment fails to detonate
July 1983	An official investigation is ordered into Father Jerzy's alleged "abuse of freedom of conscience and religion"
February 1984	Receives a rosary from Polish pope, John Paul II
October 19, 1984	Celebrates his last Mass
October 29, 1984	Father Jerzy's body is found in the waters of the Wloclawek Reservoir
November 2, 1984	Two hundred thousand mourners turn out for Father Jerzy's burial. A martyr for Solidarity is born

October 1985   The trial of Father Jerzy's murderers is televised nationally

Further Reading

Boyes, Roger and John Moody. *The Priest Who Had to Die.* London: V. Gollanz, 1986. Recounts the political events leading up to the disappearance of Father Jerzy, and the effect of his death on the Solidarity movement.

Harwood, Ronald. *The Deliberate Death of a Polish Priest.* Oxford, England: Amber Lane Press, 1985. A 60-page play based on the transcripts of the trial and other material concerning the murder of Father Jerzy.

Sikorska, Grazyna. *A Martyr for the Truth: Jerzy Popieluszko.* Grand Rapids, Mich.: Eerdmans Publishing, 1985. A native of Poland, the author concentrates on the faith and self-sacrifice of Father Jerzy, with less attention to the political aspects.

Laszlo Tokes's stand against communism ignited the one-week revolution that overthrew the Ceausescu regime. (James Colburn Photoreporters)

Pastor Laszlo Tokes

Almost by accident, the Reverend Laszlo Tokes (To-kes) lit the spark that overthrew the Communist government in Romania, one of the most repressive regimes in any country in the world. For speaking out against the Communists during his sharp-tongued Sunday sermons, the 37-year-old clergyman suffered years of harrassment. In late 1989 when Tokes was ordered to leave his small church and refused, a crowd of loyal supporters gathered outside the church. The police arrived, arrested Reverend Tokes, and dragged him and his pregnant wife away to a guarded church in a remote province.

Having fallen into the hands of the Communists, Reverend Tokes was wrongly presumed dead. Angry crowds swelled in his home province of Transylvania, and the tempest soon spread to the capital city, Bucharest. The crackdown on Tokes had inspired these demonstrations across the nation. In just a matter of days, the Communist regime was overthrown, President Nicolae Ceausescu and his wife Elena lay dead, and Tokes quietly returned to the priesthood.

Laszlo Tokes was born on April 1, 1952, in Kolozsvar, in northern Transylvania, where his family was part of the large Hungarian minority population in Romanian Transylvania. His father was a pastor in the Hungarian Reformed Church and was very poor. Laszlo's parents lived with their six children in an apartment on the church courtyard.

It was a difficult birth. His mother's history of heart problems and poor health during her pregnancy took a heavy toll on her newborn. Laszlo's first few minutes of life were spent with frantic nurses pounding on his chest to start his heart beating again. The infant survived, and his childhood was a happy one.

His siblings always teased him good-naturedly for having been born on April Fools' Day. When Laszlo indicated at a young age that he might want to be a bishop someday, his brothers and sisters laughed uncontrollably. "Bishops aren't born on All Fools' Day," they said.

One of young Laszlo's earliest memories was of the Soviet invasion of Hungary in 1956. He sat with his family listening to the hourly radio reports. For the first time in his life he had an inkling of the tragedies of the Hungarian people.

Though he was Hungarian, there were still a few schools in Kolozsvar that were Hungarian Protestant. Because their students spoke Hungarian, the schools had held out against the policy of the government to make the language and culture of Romania compulsory for the whole country. In officially atheistic Romania, Laszlo attended a primary school that had been a Hungarian Reformed School and a secondary school founded by Hungarian Catholics.

His mother secretly longed for at least one of her sons to become a church pastor. But she never pressured them, and she showed no disappointment at all as her sons chose vocations in other fields. Thus it was a very special moment for her when, in his mid-teens, Laszlo came to her and announced, "I am going to be a pastor."

The clergy was not a very practical career choice in Communist Romania. The education policy of the country did not recognize the Christian ministry as a useful calling. Though the priesthood was tolerated, the government strongly discouraged students from entering it. Many pupils in Romanian schools who hoped to prepare for the priesthood at Church seminaries kept their plans a secret. Even the director of Laszlo's school laughed uproariously when he heard about Laszlo's ambition.

The call to the ministry had not turned Laszlo into a saint. As a teenager, he was susceptible to the phases of rebellion and independence that all teenagers go through. In his final year of school, at the age of 17, he changed his mind about becoming a minister. He felt unsure that he was fit to counsel other people when he was not perfect himself. Then he changed his mind again and decided on becoming a minister in the Hungarian Reformed Church in Romania.

The only Reformed theological college in Romania was the Kolozsvar Theological Institute. It was a famous institute with a great tradition. But in the 1950s, it was essentially dismantled. The building and school remained, but the Communist regime made wholesale changes to the staff. The regime installed its own puppets—weak conformists who were appointed and paid by the state. Teachers were compromised before they ever entered the classroom and were without moral or professional commitment.

When Tokes entered the college in 1971, he enjoyed student life, but was appalled by the quality of the teaching. The reason was obvious. It was never intended that the students should leave the institute properly equipped to preach. The teachers presented the life of Jesus Christ as a mere theological topic, without exploring the meaning of His life, that Jesus was a revolutionary who stood up for the oppressed. Such teachings might have inspired the masses to rise up against the government. Eventually, Reverend Tokes's teachings did.

At first, as a student, Tokes lived at home and made the short journey to the university each day on foot. But after a while he asked his parents if he could move into a dormitory.

"Why?" asked his mother. "It's so expensive." Tokes answered confidently, "I want to live with the other students. We need to be together to make a stand." His mother understood. The need for the student body to have an identity and a voice was becoming very clear.

In the late 1960s and early 1970s the Romanian government's pressure on the Hungarian population was beginning to intensify. The government's record of persecution against Protestants and other denominations was well known. At the same time there was a rapid deterioration in the government's treatment of the Hungarian community in Transylvania. Human rights abuses were mounting. When Tokes entered the Theological Institute, he found himself engaged in the first of his own conflicts with the regime—on two counts: as a member of the Hungarian minority and as a man of the cloth.

At the Theological Institute in Kolozsvar there were two students with whom Tokes became especially close friends. Together the three decided to do something about the desperate situation in the Church. They refused to follow the prescribed path. Instead, they started asking questions of the authorites at the institute. First they wanted a properly elected student government in the institute, instead of one appointed by the administration. They also wanted to know why there was an inadequate supply of books. Finally, they demanded to know why there were plainclothes spies from the government in their classrooms, some of them members of their own student body. The practice of placing spies in classrooms was a well-known tradition at the institute. Tokes was never punished for his actions, perhaps because his father was a prominent minister. Only later would he learn that everything he did was placed in the government's political dossier.

In the Hungarian Reformed Church, theology students are required to spend two years in a training post after completing their formal studies. When Tokes and his two friends discussed their strategy for changing the Church, they looked to the smallest deanery in the diocese of Kolozsvar. It was in Brasov, a city to the east in a predominantly German area of Romania. The three decided that Tokes should apply to go to Brasov on graduation in 1975. Because it was a small parish, they thought Tokes would find it easier there to change the Church from within.

In the month after he arrived in Brasov, Reverend Tokes was called to the headquarters of the Securitate, the Romanian secret police. "We wished to make your acquaintance, Mr. Tokes. Welcome to Brasov," the officer said, pulling a complete dossier from his files. The dossier covered Tokes's activities for the past four years at the seminary. Apparently Tokes was already branded a dissident.

In Brasov he asked his bishop for Hungarian Bibles, books, and religious literature for his younger parishioners. Under the Romanian dictatorship, however, simply educating people about Hungarian history was considered dissent. To create uniform loyalty among Romania's various ethnic groups, including 1.7 million Hungarians and 200,000 Germans, Ceausescu was waging what his enemies called "cultural genocide." No cause was more important to Tokes than the government's deplorable treatment of his fellow ethnic Hungarians, who made up 8 percent of the Romanian population.

Despite being observed by the Securitate, whose spies were everywhere in Romania, Tokes went about his business as the assistant to two pastors, at two Reformed churches in Brasov. He spent two happy years. Tokes had a good relationship with the Brasov pastors and a job to do that was clearly necessary. But when the two years were up it was time to move on.

In 1977 more serious trouble began when Tokes was transferred to Dej, another small town in Transylvania, to work as assistant pastor. A large part of Tokes's time was spent working with young people. He started a Bible group with about 120 members who met weekly. By meeting with this group, he defiantly mixed Bible study with Hungarian folklore, which was enough to provoke the authorities.

Tokes had no dreams of toppling the regime or launching a revolution. That seemed impossible. Communism in Romania was a complex system of government control and information networks that kept everyone spying on one another. It was a totalitarian system unrivaled in almost any other country in the world. Tokes dreamed only of cleansing the Church from within and using it as a base to venture out against the monolith of the Communist state. He wanted to bring scripture out of the shadow of the state.

To make these changes, he had to challenge the Church leadership directly. He was young, impatient, and angry with his own Church. So he began to write letters. He wrote to every pastor in the diocese asking how many hymn books and Bibles he had in his church and castigating the turncoat nature of the Church leaders.

Tokes began to involve himself in journalism. He contributed to the samizdat, or underground newspapers, which were becoming an important phenomenon in Eastern Europe in the early 1970s. In Dej a group of friends started an underground newspaper called *Counterpoints*. Tokes contributed articles discussing the terrible state of the Church. He and his friends knew it was only a matter of time before the Securitate discovered the newspaper and its contributors.

In 1983 the Securitate finally cracked down on *Counterpoints*. Tokes's involvement with the newspaper, particularly his claims that the Church was corrupt and guilty of collaboration with the Communist authorities, made life difficult for him in many ways. The Securitate increased their harassment, and in 1984, after the congregation elected Tokes as pastor, the state initiated proceedings against him. The Securitate charged him with questioning the quality of the Church resources and slandering Church leaders.

Tokes was found guilty and demoted to assistant pastor. Soon after that he received a letter from the Church informing him that he was to be transferred to the tiny village of Uzdiszentpeter, 50 miles from Kolozsvar. Tokes refused to accept the decision of Bishop Nagy, and explained his refusal in a letter to the bishop. The case attracted a great deal of publicity, mainly because Tokes stayed where he was, in Dej. Eventually he was dismissed from the priesthood by the Church.

While in Dej after he had been expelled from the pastorship, Tokes decided to marry a woman named Edith Joo. They had known each other since Tokes first arrived in Dej, and they had become close friends. Though he never intended to marry, their friendship had deepened and, in 1985, they decided to marry. The wedding was a major local event. All the people from the church were invited to attend. There were about 300 guests at the wedding and at the reception. Of course, the Securitate found it all extremely interesting that a dismissed priest was so popular among the people. They took photographs and made notes during the speeches.

Defrocked from the priesthood, Tokes and his wife went home to Kolozsvar, to live at his parents' house. At the time, as it happened, Tokes's father was speaking out against the government too. As a deputy bishop and a professor, the elder Tokes had long been appalled by the condition of the Church. Tokes and his father became more determined than ever to fight against the regime. They wrote to every forum of discussion in the country. They wrote to the Church and also to the Communist Party. Tokes himself even wrote to the leader of the country, Ceausescu. Of course, Ceausescu did not reply.

Every day Tokes donned his black vestments and went to the bishop's palace in Kolozsvar. There he would sit from eight o'clock in the morning until four o'clock in the afternoon to protest his expulsion. For two years he was unemployed. In 1986 a review committee finally reconsidered his case and reinstated him as an ordained minister in the Hungarian Reformed Church. In June 1986 he took the post of assistant pastor in Timisoara, Transylvania, the country's westernmost region, where most of Romania's ethnic Hungarians were concentrated.

The appointment was a very clever attempt to silence Tokes. Timisoara was a town far away from Kolozsvar, on the Yugoslavian border. Leo Peuker, the pastor whom Tokes was to assist, had been a known informer for the Securitate and a collaborator with the Ceausescu regime. From day to day and from week to week, Peuker reported on all of Tokes's activities—what he had been doing, to whom he had been talking, and what he said. In effect, Tokes was in ecclesiastical exile.

Though the small congregation was afraid of Peuker and his links with the Securitate, most of them were outraged by the way Tokes and his wife Edith were being treated. Their first child, a son named Mate, had been born that winter, and the young family was living in a cramped single room. With no firewood, the cold penetrated into every corner of the room. Tokes feared that his baby would become ill if something were not done immediately. There was a larger apartment downstairs in their building that was empty but they were not allowed to move into it.

While their situation was growing worse, Reverend Peuker died shortly after Christmas. The congregation saw the hand of God in his death and elected Tokes as his successor. Tokes was approved by Bishop Papp, with one proviso. "It is a probationary post," Papp warned him. "Your appointment as full pastor will be confirmed if all goes well. It all depends on how you conduct yourself." Bishop Papp and his Securitate colleagues had tried once to drive

Tokes out of the priesthood. Now they were trying another tack. By dangling promises of advancement and a glittering future in front of him, they hoped to keep him quiet. They were mistaken. Tokes was determined not to settle into the same comfortable rut as his predecessor. As a result, the congregation grew steadily—and Tokes continued his efforts to educate them about the government's attempts to stifle any expressions of Hungarian culture.

Tokes's actions were noted by the Church authorities. After two years, Tokes was summoned repeatedly to the bishop's palace in Nagyvarad to explain his successes. He was accused by the bishop of the monstrous crime of allowing the membership of his church to grow too quickly. "You are drawing too much attention to the Church," Tokes was told.

Tokes knew he could get into trouble but he did not let up. No cause aroused his wrath more than the plight of his fellow ethnic Hungarians. Tokes ran afoul of the authorities again when he attacked the government's plan to raze up to 8,000 villages and resettle their residents in high-rise apartment complexes. Some 50,000 ethnic Hungarians would be relocated under the program. The cultural consequences were clear to Tokes. Communities that had grown up over centuries would disappear in days. An entire way of life would vanish.

Among Tokes's demands were that no church be demolished without being replaced by another church. A document to this effect was sent to Bishop Papp. Tokes did not have to wait long for his response. On September 12, 1988, Tokes was again summoned to the office of Bishop Papp to be disciplined. Tokes ignored the bishop's threats. Finally, on March 20, 1989, he received word from the bishop that he would be dismissed from his pastorship at Timisoara. He was told to vacate his church and move to Mineu, a tiny village in the mountains to the north of Kolozsvar, far away from Timisoara, where he would have a new congregation.

The Church and the government found it difficult to silence Tokes. He was still on probation, but expulsion would have provoked a Church incident and considerable interest in the West. Refusal to accept a bishop's instruction, however, would look like deliberate disobedience by Tokes. But Tokes knew that the prospects for his congregation were bleak if he were removed. He knew that Papp would ensure that the next pastor was compliant and willing to return his church to its old ways.

Tokes wrote the bishop a letter saying that he would agree only to house arrest. He said he would leave his flat only to carry out his duties as a pastor. Tokes added that he would resist any attempt to remove him from his church by any means. "I only ask one thing: leave me in peace to carry on my work, and do not curtail our freedom that is ensured by the Constitution, the statutes and my contract."

For the next eight months, Tokes resisted at home while both the Church and government authorities tried to evict him. Tokes continued to work with his church. In April, Kossuth Radio in Hungary transmitted a special Sunday service in which they read the contents of Tokes's letter to the bishop. Tokes's conflict with the Church was known throughout Transylvania. During the summer, Hungarian Radio broadcast at least one item about Tokes and his church every week. Radio Free Europe, Voice of America, and the BBC World Service carried reports that spread the word throughout Romania.

> "I only ask one thing: leave me in peace to carry on my work, and do not curtail our freedom that is ensured by the Constitution, the statutes and my contract."

Millions in western Romania heard Tokes speak when he granted an interview to a Hungarian current affairs television program. The interview was aired in July and was picked up across the border in Romania. Tokes spoke about the effects of Ceausescu's policies on all of Romania—the deliberate attempt to eradicate minority cultures, the mass movement of people to the cities, the interference in and manipulation of the churches by the regime.

Tokes's struggle had gone far beyond the issue of religious freedom. He was now taking on the national government. For taking aim at the government itself, many dissenters in Romania had been ruthlessly eliminated. It was entirely possible that Tokes might be the next unexplained casualty. In fact, the number of anonymous telephone threats steadily increased. They all bore the same message: If Tokes did not cooperate, he would be in great personal danger. Still he pressed on.

Tokes was pushing against the barriers of an unjust government. He was testing the limits of protest, and the consequences were severe. Securitate guards were placed at the entrance to the church building. Visitors to the church were cross-examined and searched, but they kept coming to church, a testament to Tokes's enormous popularity. On August 15 Tokes sent an open letter to Papp calling on him "to resign your title of bishop, to which you have no claim." Ten days later the bishop's response came. The brief note informed Tokes that he was no longer a pastor of the Reformed Church. The terse letter stated that Tokes would have to vacate his apartment by December 15. Pinned to the letter was the notice of eviction.

Tokes was not surprised. He and the bishop had been locked in confrontation for years. The young pastor's offense: complaining about a shortage of hymn books; organizing youth activities in the church; protesting against the destruction of the Romanian villages; appearing on a foreign television program and speaking against the brutal oppression of Ceausescu's regime. Bishop Papp, who had always been considered a corrupt bishop who catered to the whims of the Communist Party, hoped to silence Tokes permanently.

As of August 20 Tokes was no longer pastor in Timisoara. Another minister would be sent to replace him. Tokes's transfer to Mineu, the isolated mountain village, was again being pressed on him. In the meantime, he was denied a ration book from the Church, leaving him unable to buy bread, meat, or fuel. Parishioners who tried to bring him provisions were confronted by police. Tokes was barred from meeting relatives. His telephone was turned off. And in the most ingenious form of harassment, authorities occasionally restored service. Periodically the phone would ring and Tokes would hear a death threat. Later he would receive bills for these incoming calls at long-distance rates.

On November 2, 1989, Tokes was sitting with his pregnant wife and his four-year-old son Mate in the small living room of their apartment when he heard a loud crash at the door. Four masked thugs broke in and came after the minister. They slashed his forehead with a knife. Edith ran into the bedroom with young Mate, but was pursued by two of the men. Tokes fought back with chairs, bottles, and whatever he could find. Two friends who were acting as Tokes's bodyguards rushed into the room and drove off the attackers. The frightening assault was over in minutes.

Tokes never learned the identities of his attackers. He was sure, though, that if they weren't members of the secret police, they were surely acting with its approval. He was also sure that the men had intended to kill him. In a smuggled videotape made that fall, a haggard Tokes showed clear signs of strain. "They've broken our windows every day," he said. "Now they've started breaking them in the church as well. Our friends sleep here now. The nights are terrible."

The authorities had sent him a pretty clear message. To stay in his church would cost Tokes his life. In December he sent his son to stay with his grandparents for the Christmas holiday. On December 10, the final Sunday before he was to be forcibly removed from his home and dismissed as a pastor of the Hungarian Reformed Church, Tokes approached the pulpit with a heavy heart.

"Dear brothers and sisters in Christ," he said. "I have been issued with a summons of eviction. I will not accept it, so I will be taken by force next Friday." When Tokes made his statement, he knew that sitting among the congregation were plainclothes Securitate officers, but still he added: "Please, come next Friday and be witnesses to what will happen. Come, be peaceful, but be witnesses."

As the people filed out of the church, Tokes wondered how many of them would turn up next Friday. Very few, he guessed, would be there to support him. Doing so would brand them "enemies of the state" like Tokes. Yet on Friday dozens of his parishioners stood in small groups of three or four and waited outside the church rectory. Tokes appeared at the window of his home and made a sign with his arm for them to come forward. About 30 parishioners moved to the window to see their beloved pastor. Although they did not know it then, they all had taken the first step in the Romanian Revolution.

Many old men and women who had not yet gone to work were among the parishioners. Church members, mingling with secret police guards, now thronged the entrance to the church. Tokes's apartment was on the first floor and the church hall itself was on the second. The front door of the apartment led to stone

"Dear brothers and sisters in Christ. I have been issued with a summons of eviction. I will not accept it, so I will be taken by force next Friday."

steps that descended to the main entrance on the side street. Church members were now thronging that entrance, interspersed with Securitate guards. The situation was a standoff. As far as the authorities knew, Tokes might be planning to leave peacefully later in the day. A forced entry into the apartment might provoke a reaction from the angry crowd. As the crowd grew, the Securitate police made a halfhearted attempt to impose control. Eventually, for some unknown reason, the guards left. For the first time in months, Tokes's apartment was unguarded.

Meanwhile, the people stayed. A flood of food, meat, milk, loaves of bread, fresh fruit, and bags of firewood kept passing through the window from Tokes's faithful parishioners. In the afternoon, the nature of the crowd changed. Students began to arrive, both Romanians and ethnic Hungarians. Tokes addressed the crowd several times, in Hungarian and then in Romanian. "We are one in Christ," he said. "We speak different languages, but we have the same Bible and the same God."

As Tokes spoke, people were praying openly in the streets. Tokes was besieged by requests from people who wanted to spend the night in his apartment. Many were people he'd never met. The members of his church tried to calm the crowd, arranging themselves in a circle to protect the entrance and to decide who should be allowed in and out. Tokes himself appealed for restraint. But as soon as he turned away from the window the chanting began again. "Tokes! Laszlo Tokes! We want Laszlo Tokes!" Tokes was moved by the massive show of support, but suddenly he felt afraid of the crowd. He wondered whether he could control them.

It was 10 o'clock. He was having supper in the kitchen with several of his close friends when a delegation appeared. It was made up of the town mayor and several colleagues. The crowd grew angry at the sight of them, suspecting that the delegation was there to secretly evict Tokes. Tokes feared that the mayor would be lynched. He tried to appeal to the crowd for reason. The crowd agreed to let the mayor enter the building on the condition that a delegation from the crowd come too, as witnesses. The mayor promised to fix the broken windows and to send a doctor to see Tokes's pregnant wife.

After the mayor left, the crowd settled down a bit. Tokes closed his windows. Meanwhile, as on the previous night, the people lit candles, and some were singing hymns. There were Securitate officers in the crowd, observing, but they could do very little without resorting to force, which might inflame the protesters. Around the church, people joined hands again in a human chain of symbolic defense. Then the crowd began shouting defiant words. "Down with Ceausescu! Down with the regime! Down with Communism."

The situation changed irrevocably at that point. The crowd did not want to listen to Tokes anymore, and the minister had no idea how long the authorities would allow the demonstrations to go on. One young demonstrator was standing near the window. Tokes did not know who he was. He was arguing with Securitate officers. Suddenly the officers began punching the demonstrator and beating him with sticks. He was covered with blood and unconscious long before they stopped their attack.

The crowd exploded and divided, with the largest group heading for the center of Timisoara. The angry mob descended on party headquarters and began breaking all the windows. Police arrived and forced the demonstrators back toward Tokes's church, and then turned a water cannon on them. Suddenly, the crowd surged forward and seized the water cannon machine, breaking it up and throwing the pieces into the nearby Bega River. More violence followed that night. They smashed store windows. They broke into a bookshop, seized all of Ceausescu's books and burned them.

Tokes could only wait and pray for peace. He had no idea what was happening outside his rectory, but it sounded as if the country had exploded into a paroxysm of violence. From his window he could see fires starting in the distance and hear the sound of breaking glass. Elsewhere in the city, the protests grew more extreme. By midnight there was relative silence. Tokes thought he could hear sporadic gunfire off in the distance. At three o'clock in the morning, the Securitate smashed each one of the windows in his house.

Nothing could stop his eviction now. A very large uniformed Securitate officer entered his apartment, stood before him, and punched a white-gloved fist into his stomach. Tokes was beaten brutally, his face covered with blood. Then he was dragged down to his office, while being punched in the face, and forced to sign the eviction papers.

It was pouring rain in the middle of the night when Tokes was driven off in a cordon of cars to the Securitate headquarters downtown. At the front of the building, partly covered, was a row of dead bodies—demonstrators who had been gunned down by the Securitate. Tokes sat in the car for 10 minutes before the driver returned. Then the cars drove off, traveling east, stopping at several checkpoints along the way. Tokes and his wife were taken in separate cars to his new parish in Mineu and put under house arrest.

There in Mineu, luckily, they found a small radio in the house and were able to keep abreast of the news. What they heard encouraged them both. At first there were only fragments of the story. Something had happened in Timisoara, but they didn't know what. As they listened intently to the radio reports, they learned that the fighting had spread to the capital city of Bucharest. Tokes and his wife were gripped with remorse over the bloodshed that was taking place all over the country—all a result of his refusal to leave his church. Now in his new apartment in Mineu, he hunkered down with Edith, listening closely to the radio reports.

Because of the government's control of communications, he didn't know what to believe.

Apparently, the Romanian revolution had begun four days earlier, on December 17, when the security police in the city of Timisoara finally moved against Tokes. Within an hour as many as 10,000 demonstrators were met by tanks and armed security forces. But unlike the bloodless revolutions in the rest of the Warsaw Pact countries, the Romanian convulsion was soaked in blood.

Tokes learned that after a barrage of warning shots, the security forces in Timisoara mowed down a line of children standing in front of a crowd. Then they turned their guns on the adults. At least 2,000 men, women, and children were killed. Three days after the massacre in Timisoara, demonstrators shouting "Give us our dead!" filled the city's blood-stained streets. As word of the killing spread, marchers turned out in towns throughout the country.

Although the Securitate interrogated Tokes and his wife mercilessly for three days in Mineu, they didn't torture them. "They wanted me to appear on TV and confess my sins during a show trial," he said later. "My wife and I were to admit we were agents of Western capitalism." On Wednesday, the interrogator stopped talking and turned on the radio. Tokes listened intently as Ceausescu, just back from Iran that day, addressed the nation.

It was clear to Tokes, as he listened to the address, that after 24 years Ceausescu had no intention of relinquishing rule. The dictator had always maintained that reform would come to Romania "when pears grow on poplar trees." Now in Bucharest he had assembled thousands of workers to applaud and wave flags on cue. Addressing the crowd from the balcony of his grandiose palace, he tried to blame the riots on ethnic Hungarian "revanchists" bent on recapturing Transylvania and returning it to Hungary.

Ceausescu was speaking of "the freedom and life of our people" when the crowd suddenly drowned him out with boos, jeers, and demands for the truth. They wanted to know the fate of Reverend Tokes and the truth about the bloody massacre in Timisoara. Visibly astonished by this face-to-face encounter with rebellion, Ceausescu froze. He quickly ended the rally and disappeared indoors. As he did so, the crowd of protesters in the square poured into the streets.

The crowd swelled to thousands. Shouts of "Freedom!" and "Down with Ceausescu!" rang out. At least 13 people were shot in the square. The streets did not clear, however, and more people were shot during the night. Angry mobs smashed store windows and besieged party headquarters and police stations. By the next day it looked as if the end was near for the dictatorship. Regular army troops were now siding with the protesters and overwhelming Ceausescu's loyal militia, the 180,000-strong Securitate, in bloody street battles.

Holed up in Mineu, Tokes later learned what happened on that bloody day in Bucharest. As the fighting intensified, Ceausescu's fate was apparently sealed at a meeting with his security chiefs. There seemed to be a split among the Securitate commanders, with only a minority favoring a continued crackdown. With his defenses crumbling, Ceausescu and his wife Elena fled. Rioters were now pouring into the presidential palace. After Ceausescu's fall, Romanian television said that Tokes was alive and well and "calling on people not to give up their fight for freedom."

When Tokes heard that Ceausescu had been arrested, he later said, "It was the happiest hour of our lives. We knew we had escaped death." Nevertheless, the expelled pastor's immediate reaction was one of disbelief. He didn't know exactly what to do with himself. His interrogators had already fled Mineu. Relatives who had driven to Mineu to join the couple now drove them to the Securitate headquarters.

U.S. Secretary of State James Baker gestures when stating that Protestant priest Laszlo Tokes sparked the December uprising that ousted former ruler Ceausescu. (AP/Wide World Photos)

When Tokes presented himself, his old interrogators were subdued. Says Tokes: "They shook hands with us and told us very politely that we were now free to go."

Back at the church in Mineu, the whole village was celebrating. It was a festive event, with people bringing food and wine to their new minister, the hero of the Romanian Revolution. Families took photographs. Everyone listened to hourly radio broadcasts of the news. Several times before nightfall Tokes said Mass. He preached from the Bible's 16th chapter of Isaiah, which speaks of the fall of tyrants and the day of the Lord's blessing. The worshiping continued for four days.

By Friday, Tokes was deluged by reporters. There was still fear in the air. For days, Ceausescu and Elena had been on the run. Nobody knew where they were. As it turned out, they were captured at the airport, trying to flee the country. Ceausescu and his wife were tried on Christmas Day, four days after his arrest, and executed on the spot by army soldiers.

That Christmas Day of 1989 Tokes watched in astonishment as the Romanian television station showed a tape of the Ceausescus' two-hour trial, during which the ousted despots remained defiant to the end. A film of their bullet-ridden corpses was aired later during the same broadcast. For the first time in 40 years, Christmas was declared a public holiday. In cities all over the country, the people of Romania knelt, prayed, and wept with joy. Tokes and his wife spent Christmas 1989 in Mineu, reunited with their son Mate, before returning to their Timisoara congregation.

Many Romanians gave Tokes credit for his crucial role in the overthrow of Ceausescu, but Tokes did not want to leave the Church and become a professional politician. He knew that his true role was as a minister of God, but thought that he might be able do both. He decided to run for the Senate in Timisoara, a district where there was a large Hungarian majority. He had high hopes of winning, but the May 20 elections were a disappointment. He lost by 11,000 votes. As many as 53,000 ballots had been invalidated by the authorities.

Two weeks before the election, Tokes was installed as Bishop of Oradea. In that post, he succeeded his old tormentor, Bishop Laszlo Papp. Beginning his inaugural sermon, he quoted Isaiah: "I have redeemed you. I have summoned you by name. You are mine."

It is clear that Romania has a long way to go in its quest for democracy. But Tokes, almost by accident and through the force of his words and his message of peaceful resistance, had already brought the country quite far. With his respect for nonviolence and the rule of law, and even a degree of forgiveness for those who had abused power, he set a remarkable example for his countrymen. If that spirit is sustained, Tokes will have shown the way to the establishment of a durable democracy.

Chronology

April 1, 1952	Born in Kolozsvar
1971–75	Studies at Theological Institute in Cluj
1975–77	Works as assistant pastor in Brasov and Zernesti
1977	Transferred to Dej
1984	Removed by Bishop Nagy as assistant pastor of Dej
December 15, 1985	Marries Edith Joo in Dej
July 1986	Begins work in Timisoara parish
March 20, 1989	Informed of his suspension as pastor of Timisoara
July 24, 1989	Hungarian TV broadcasts March interview
December 15, 1989	Date set for eviction; demonstrations begin around Tokes's church
December 17, 1989	Tokes and wife Edith dragged from the church and taken to Mineu. Protests continue in Timisoara
December 21, 1989	Ceausescu speaks to rally in Bucharest. Speech interrupted after protests. Riots in capital
December 22, 1989	Ceausescus flee. National Salvation Front declares itself in power. Tokes's interrogators flee
December 25, 1989	Ceausescus tried and executed

March 29, 1990   Tokes elected bishop of Oradea
May 8, 1990   Installed as bishop

Further Reading

Corley, Felix, and John Eibner. *In the Eye of the Romanian Storm.* Old Tappan, N.J.: F.H. Revell, 1990. Puts the Romanian revolution in the context of the history of the church and Hungarian-Romanian ethnic relations. Recounts the crackdown on Tokes that inspired nationwide demonstrations that toppled Ceausescu.

Tokes, Laszlo, with David Porter. *The Fall of Tyrants.* Wheaton, Ill.: Crossway Books, 1990. The incredible story of Tokes's witness, the people of Romania, and the overthrow of Ceausescu, as seen through Tokes's own eyes.

Index

This index is designed as an aid to access the narrative text and special features. Page numbers in **boldface** indicate key topics. Page numbers in *italic* indicate illustrations or captions. A "c" following the page number indicates chronology.

A

Adamec, Ladislas   96, 98, 99
Afghanistan   1, 13, 72, 73–74, 80c
Andropov, Yuri   68, 69, 71

B

Baker, James   *169*
Baldridge, Malcolm   72
Baltic Committee for Free and Independent Trade Unions   112, 126c
Banska Bystrica, Czechoslovakia   25, 38c
Barsukov, Mikhail   57
Beria, Lavrenti   5–6
Bethe, Hans   16
Bologna University   34, 39c
Bonner, Elena   11, *12*, 13–16, *18*
Brasov, Romania   155, 171c
Bratislava, Czechoslovakia   24, 27, 34, 38c, 39c
"Bread riots" (1970) (Poland)   111
Brezhnev, Leonid   9, 45, 56, 68, 69
  and Prague Spring   30–31, 32, 38c
Bush, George   78

C

Capek, Josef   86
Ceausescu, Elena   151, *168*, 169–170, 171c
Ceausescu, Nicolae   31, 151, *157*, *161*, *165*, 167–170, 171c
Cechnya revolt (1995)   58
censorship *see glasnost*; intellectual freedom
Charter 77   91–92, 103c, 104c
Chernenko, Konstantin   70
Chrostowski, Waldemar   140, *141*
Civic Forum   96, 98, 99, 101, 104c
Coastal Worker, The (publication)   112
Collapse of Communism, The (Kaufman)   102–103
Comenius University   25
Committee for Social Self-Defense (KOR)   112, 114
Commonwealth of Independent States   78–79, 81c
communist ideology *see* Marxism-Leninism
Congress of People's Deputies (U.S.S.R.)   50, *55*, 60c, 74
Conspirators, The (Havel)   91

Counterpoints (publication)   156
Czechoslovakia
  Communist repression   94–95
  conversion to capitalism   100–101
  Dubcek role in   21–39
  Havel role in   83–105
  Slovakia split from   101–102
  Soviet invasion of   10, 21, 30–33, 38c, 89, 103c
  Velvet Revolution (1989)   21, 35–37, 39c, 83, 96–100, 104c

D

Dej, Romania   155–156, 171c
dissidents *see also specific personalities*
  Czech Charter 77   91–92, 103c, 104c
  Dubcek's eased policy toward   27
  Gorbachev's eased policy toward   15, 71
  Polish Committee for Social Self-Defense   112
  Polish Communist treatment of   137–138

173

Polish labor movement *see* Solidarity Free Trade Union
Popieluszko's martyrdom 129
Romania's Hungarian minority as 155, 161
Sakharov declarations 8, 9, 10
Soviet treatment of 1, 9, 13–15, 34
Walesa and Gdansk Shipyard as symbol for 114
Dubcek, Alexander 20, **21–39**
background and youth 22–23, 37c
honorary degree 34, 39c
return as pro-democracy leader 35–37, 39c
rise in Slovak Communist party 24–26, 37c, 38c
Dubcek, Anna Ondrisova 24, 34, 37c

E

East Germany 72, 95
economic restructuring *see* perestroika

G

Garden Party, The (Havel) 88, 103c
Gdansk Shipyard (Poland) 107, 110–115, 133, 134
genetics 7–8
Gierek, Edward 111
glasnost (openness)
Czech dissidents and 94
Gorbachev's initiation of 71, 79
hard-line conservatives and 41, 76
Sakharov criticism of pace of 16
Yeltsin "confession" in context of 48–49
Gorbachev, Mikhail 62, **63–81**
background and youth 64–66, *80*
and collapse of East European communism 95–96
coup attempt against (1991) 52–54, 60c, 63, 76–77, 81c
decline in popularity and power 71, 75–79
eased policies toward Czechoslovakia 34, 35, 94
eased policy toward Poland 120, 122
marriage 67, 80c
Nobel Peace Prize to 75
political legacy of 79
presidency of Soviet Union 60, 81c
presidency resignation 61, 78
reform policies *see glasnost*; *perestroika*
rise in Communist Party 65, 68–71, 80c
Sakharov relationship 15, 16, 19c, 71
Yeltsin relationship 41, 45–48, 50, 51, 52, 54–55, 73, 75–78
Gorbachev, Raisa Titornko 67
Gorbachev and After (White) 79
Gorki, U.S.S.R.
Dubcek family move to 23, 37c
Sakharovs' exile in 1, 13–14, 18c
gulags (labor camps) 9

H

Havel, Olga Splichalova 86, 87, 90, 93, 103c
Havel, Vaclav 82, **83–105**, 99
arrests of 90, 92–93, 94, 95
assessment of 102–103
background and youth 84–87, 103c
Czech presidency 37–38, 39c, 83, 99–102, 104c
health problems 93
marriage 86, 103c
personal popularity 102
plays and essays 86–89, 91, 93, 94, 103c
refusal to defect 92
trial and imprisonment 92–93, 104c
Velvet Revolution leadership 35, 96–100
Hitler, Adolf 23, 108
House of Writers (Prague) 87, 103c
human rights 11, 13, 89, 91, 104c
Hungarian ethnics (in Romania) 154, 155, 158–159, 167
Hungarian Reformed Church 151–160, 163, 170
Hungary 30, 34, 95, 152
Husak, Gustav 33, 91, 96
hydrogen bomb, first 1, 4, 6, 18c

I

Ignatievich, Nikolai 41, 42
Increased Difficulty of Concentration, The (Havel) 89, 103c
intellectual freedom *see also glasnost*
    Czech Communist position on 92
    Father Jerzy Popieluszko's sermon on 135–136
    Sakharov's championship of 9, 10–11, 13, 16
Izvestia (newspaper) 138

J

Jagielski, Mieczyslaw 114
Jakes, Milos 34, 36, 96, 97, 104c
Jaruzelski, Wojciech 117, 122, 123, 127c, 141, 144
John Paul II, Pope 113, 117–118, 119, 133, 138, 141–142, 148c
"Just a Few Sentences" (Havel) 95

K

Kaufman, Michael T. 102–103
Khrushchev, Nikita 8, 9, 25, 69
KOR *see* Committee for Social Self-Defense
Kraszewski, Bishop 138

L

labor camps (*gulags*) 9
labor unions, 114–116, 126c *see also* Solidarity Free Trade Union
Largo Desolato (Havel) 93
Lech Walesa and Poland (Vnenchak) 125
Lenin Shipyard *see* Gdansk Shipyard
"Letters to Olga" (Havel) 104c
Lysenko, Trofim 8, 9

M

Marxism-Leninism
    Dubcek's study of 25
    Gorbachev's belief in 67
    Havel's satires on 88, 89, 91
    Sakharov's view of 3
Masses for the Country 135, 137, 138, 145, 148c
Mazowiecki, Tadeusz 123, 124
Memorandum, The (Havel) 88–89, 103c
Miller, Craig 59
miners' strike (Silesia) 120, 122
Mlynar, Zdenek 66
Moscow News (publication) 35
Moscow State University 3, 18c, 49, 65–66, 80c
Mountain Hotel, The (Havel) 91

N

Nagy, Bishop 157, 171c
Navratilova, Martina 100
New York Times (newspaper) 10, 16
Nobel Peace Prize
    to Gorbachev 75
    to Sakharov 11, 13, 18c
    to Walesa 118
Novotny, Antonin 25, 26, 38c
Nuclear Test Ban Treaty (1963) 8
nuclear weapons
    first atomic bomb 5
    first hydrogen bomb 1, 4, 6, 18c
    Gorbachev-Bush cuts 78
    Russian control of Soviet arsenal 79
    Sakharov's criticism of 1–2, 7–8
    Soviet moratorium (1985) 72
    testing 7–8

P

Palach, Jan 95
Papp, Joseph 89
Papp, Bishop Laszlo 150, 158–159, 161–162
perestroika (economic restructuring)
    conservative resistance to 47
    Gorbachev implementation of 63, 71–76, 79, 80c
    and revised view of dissidents 15, 35
    Walesa critique of 120
    Yeltsin support for 41
Peuker, Leo 158
Piotrowski, Grzegorz 145
Poland
    democratic elections 122–124, 127c, 146
    fall of Communist regime 95, 123–124, 127c
    John Paul II's visits 113, 118, 133
    martial law 117, 135–136, 148c
    Popieluszko role in 129–149
    trial of Father Jerzy's murderer 144–146, 149c
    Walesa role in 107–127

worker militancy *see*
    Solidarity Free Trade
    Union
Popieluszko, Father Jerzy
    128, **129–149**, *139*
  background and
    youth   130–131,
    147c
  health problems   132,
    133, 148c
  kidnapping and murder of   129,
    140–142, 148c
  legacy of   146–147
  Masses for the Country   135, 137, 138,
    145, 148c
  trial of murderers
    144–145, 149c
Prague, Czechoslovakia
  anticommunist underground   85
  Havel's youth in
    84–85, 103c
  pro-democracy demonstrations   35, 94,
    96, 104c
  Soviet tanks in
    (1968)   32, 33
Prague Spring (1968)
  9–10, 21–22, 29–33,
  35, 37, 89, 95, 103c,
  104c
Pravda (newspaper)   48

R

Radio Free Europe   89,
    160
Reagan, Ronald   72, 80c,
    144
Red Brigades   117
Reed, Lou   100
*Reflections on Progress,
    Coexsistence and Intellectual Freedom* (Sakharov)   10, 18c
Rolling Stones   100
Roman Catholic Church
    109, 110, 113, 114,
    117–119, 129–147,
    145, 148c

Romania
  Hungarian minority
    154, 155, 158–159
  revolt against
    Ceausescu   151,
    163–165, 167–168,
    169, 171c
  Tokes role in
    151–172
Russian Orthodox
    Church   52–53
Russian Republic
  Cechnya revolt   58
  discontent in   55–56
  elections   51, 55, 58,
    60c, 61c, 76
  Gorbachev's unpopularity in   79
  Russian White House   52,
    53, 54, 57, 61c, 76

S

St. Stanislaw Kostka
    Church (Warsaw)
    133–137, 141,
    142–143, 145, 148c
Sakharov, Andrei *xiv*,
    1–19, *12*, *17*
  background and
    youth   2–3, 18c
  death of   16
  on Dubcek's heroism
    37
  on human freedoms
    10–11, 18c
  hunger strikes   11, 14
  hydrogen bomb design   1, 4, 6, 18c
  internal exile   1,
    13–14, 18c
  marriages   4, 11, 18c
  Nobel Peace Prize to
    11, 13
  return from exile   15,
    16, 19c, 71
Salisbury, Harrison E.   16
samizdat   156
Scharansky, Anatoly   71
Seifert, Jaroslav   85
Shawcross, William   37
Sikorska, Grazyna   147

Silesian miners' strike
    120, 122
Slovakia
  Dubcek's background
    in   21, 23–26, 36,
    37c
  independence as Slovak Republic
    101–102
Sofiano, Yekaterina   2
Solidarity Free Trade Union
  banning of (1981)
    117, 118, 122, 135
  legalization and election victories
    (1989)   107,
    122–124, 127c
  Popieluszko as martyr
    of   129, 133–134,
    143, 146, 148c
  registration as independent trade union   114–116, 126c
Solidarity Weekly (publication)   118
Soviet Academy of Sciences   4, 7, 11, 18c
Soviet Union *see also* Russian Republic
  Afghanistan occupation by   1, 13, 72,
    73–74, 80c
  arms control   8, 72,
    78
  coup attempt against
    Gorbachev   52–54,
    60c, 63, 76–77, 81c
  dissolution of   55,
    61c, 78, 81c
  Dubcek's early years
    in   22–23
  first hydrogen bomb
    1, 4, 6, 18c
  first multiparty free
    election   50–51, 74
  formal opposition legitimization   16
  Gorbachev role in
    63–81

invasion of Czechoslovakia *see* Prague Spring
liberalization policies *see glasnost*; *perestroika*
Sakharov role in 1–19
Stalinist purges 23
treatment of dissidents 1, 9, 13–15, 34
"war of presidents" 51, 52, 63, 73, 75–76
Yeltsin role in 41–61
Stalin, Joseph 5, 6, 23, 25, 48, 71
steel plant strike (Warsaw) 134–135, 148c
strikes
Gdansk (1980) 107, 111, 113–115, 134
Silesian miners (1988) 120, 122
Walesa on purpose of 112
Warsaw steel plant 134–135, 148c
Supreme Soviet
approval of new legislature by 74
eligibility for 16
Gorbachev post in 68
Yeltsin decision against abolishing 55
Suslov, Mikhail A. 68, 69
Szadurski, Karol 143

T

Tamm, Igor 4, 5, 6, 7
Temptation (Havel) 94
Thatcher, Margaret 99
Theater on the Balustrade (Prague) 88, 89, 90, 103c
"Thirty-sixers" (literary group) 85

Timisoara, Romania 158–160, 162, 166–167, 168, 171c
Tokes, Edith Joo 157, 158, 162, 166, 167, 170, 171c
Tokes, Laszlo 150, **151–172**, *169*
background and youth 151–152, 153, 171c
expulsions from pastorates 157–158, 161, 163
harassment of 156–157, 162
marriage 157, 171c
resistance to Church authority 160–162
Tokes, Mate 158, 162, 163, 170
trade unions *see* labor unions; Solidarity Free Trade Union
Trencin, Slovakia 23, 38c
"Two Thousand Words" (Dubcek) 95
Tyminski, Stanislaw 124

U

Uhrovec, Slovakia 11, 37c
United States
Havel's visit to 89, 103c
Soviet relations 72, 78, 80c
Urals Heavy Pipe Construction Trust 44
Urals Polytechnic Institute 43, 59c
Urbanek, Zdenek 97
U.S.S.R. *see* Soviet Union

V

Vasilievna, Klavdia 41, 42
Velvet Revolution (1989) 21, 35, 36–37, 39c, 83, 104c

Vikhireva, Klava 4, 11, 18c
Vnenchak, Dennis 125
Voice of America 10–11, 160

W

Walesa, Danuta Golos 110, 117, 126c
Walesa, Lech 106, **107–127**, *121*
arrest and jailing of 117, 118, 135
assessment of 125–126
background and youth 108–110, 126c
on Father Jerzy's murder 141, 143, 156
Gdansk shipyard strike 107, 111–114, 133
marriage and family 110–111, 126c
negotiation skills 108, 117
Nobel Peace Prize to 118
popularity decline 124–125
presidency of Poland 107, 124–125, 127c, 146
Warsaw Letter (1968) 31
Warsaw Pact 32, 38c, 89
Warsaw steel workers' strike 134–135, 148c
Wenceslas Square (Prague) 33, 35, 36, 39c, 96–98
White, Stephen 79
White House *see* Russian White House
Wojtyla, Karol *see* John Paul II, Pope
Writers' Union (Czechoslovakia) 27
Wyszynski, Stefan 132

Y

Yeltsin, Boris 40, **41–61**
 background and youth 41–43, 59c
 blockade of parliament by 57, 61c
 and coup against Gorbachev 52–54, 60c, 63, 76–77
 "confession" of 48–49
 criticism of Gorbachev 51, 52, 63, 73, 74, 75–76, 77–78
 criticism of party leaders 46–48, 60c
 and dissolution of Soviet Union 81c
 drinking episodes 52
 election as Russian parliament leader 50–51, 60c, 74
 election/reelection as Russian president 51, 55, 58, 60c, 61c, 76
 health problems 48, 49, 58, 61c
 legacy of 58–59
 marriage and family 44, 59c
 persona of 42–43, 47, 49
 popularity base 50, 76
 rise in Communist Party 44–46, 59c
 western critics of 51–52
Yeltsin, Naya Girina 44, 59c

Z

Zappa, Frank 100
Zhirinovsky, Vladimir 58